'When you're drunk, your mouth smells funny.'

DANIEL, aged six

'Alcohol is a narcotic, like tobacco. If it didn't exist and someone invented it tomorrow, it would undoubtedly be banned.'

ROWAN ATKINSON

'When we catch a driver at eight, nine or ten in the morning who is over the limit and provides a positive breath test, they're normally shocked because they can't believe that the drink is still affecting them. They seem to think that if they've had a few hours sleep they're OK, but of course this is not the case.'

POLICE PATROLMAN

'My name is Anna, and I'm eight, and my favourite drink is champagne.'

'As a result of patients that we have in that are abusive and under the influence of alcohol, we have had panic buttons fitted into casualty.'

NURSE

'Society teaches us to expect that alcohol makes us witty and excitable, or witty and convivial, but the reality can often be very, very different.'

DR IAN ROBERTSON

'When Daddy has a glass of beer his jokes make me laugh.'

ELIZABETH, aged four

Pssst...

A REALLY USEFUL

GUIDE TO ALCOHOL

Dʀ Aʟᴀɴ Mᴀʀʏᴏɴ Dᴀᴠɪs

With an introduction by

Hᴜɢʜ Lᴀᴜʀɪᴇ

A Pan Original

PAN BOOKS London, Sydney and Auckland

First published 1989 by Pan Books Ltd,
Cavaye Place, London SW10 9PG

9 8 7 6 5 4 3 2 1

Copyright © Dr Alan Maryon Davis

Illustrations by George Sharp

ISBN 0 330 31109 3

Photoset by Parker Typesetting Service, Leicester
Printed and bound in Great Britain by
Richard Clay Ltd, Bungay, Suffolk

This book accompanies the television series *Pssst...a really useful guide to alcohol*, produced by Prospect Pictures for BBC Wales and BBC1 in association with the Health Promotion authority for Wales.

CONTENTS

INTRODUCTION BY HUGH LAURIE

I've never written a foreword before. My advisers tell me I may never write one again. I say this partly as a warning to those readers who might casually think: 'I won't bother with the foreword by Hugh Laurie, he's always writing forewords. Plenty more where this came from.' If that's what you think, then I can only say you're taking one hell of a risk. My advisers agree with me on this. One hell of a risk.

I also want you to realise that if a man's only going to write one foreword in his life, then he'd be considerably less than a man if he didn't attach it to a pretty damned important book. I believe this to be such a book. Why they didn't come right out and call it 'A Pretty Damned Important Book' beats me for over an hour with a wet pyjama cord. Still.

Alcohol. Now for heaven's sake, I'm not in the business of trying to tell people how to behave. Good Lord no. I got out of that business years ago, and bought a chain of newsagents with the proceeds. Nevertheless, I commend this book to you because it can help us all to get something out of alcohol apart from headaches, paunches, unemployed, friendless, or dead. I'd call that pretty damned important. Wouldn't you?

ACKNOWLEDGEMENTS

Firstly, very special thanks to Colin Cranleigh-Swash, an excellent writer-researcher, who assisted me in assembling the facts for this book and provided me with some original ideas for low-alcohol cocktail recipes.

Warm thanks also to Tony McAvoy of Prospect Pictures, a good friend, who produced the BBC TV series and persuaded me to write a book to accompany it.

I'd like to give a big thank you to Judith Hannam of Pan Books for her steady calmness and care in seeing the publication through in record time.

I'm grateful to Alcohol Concern, the national charitable body, for much useful information, and especially to their librarian, Roy Johnson, for his painstaking support. Similarly, I'd like to thank Andrew McNeil and Lois Brown of the Institute of Alcohol Studies for their valuable help. My gratitude also goes to Action on Alcohol Abuse, the Brewers' Society, the Scottish Health Education Group, and the Wine and Spirit Association of Great Britain for information they've provided.

Finally, thanks and much love to my wife, Anne, and daughters, Jessie and Elizabeth, for putting up with me so uncomplainingly while I spent all those hours locked in my garret, emerging only for the odd marmite sandwich and glass of low-alcohol lager.

CHEERS WITHOUT TEARS

> '*A woman drove me to drink – and I never even wrote to thank her.*'
>
> W. C. FIELDS

Nobody drinks alcohol!

We drink drinks – long drinks, short drinks, bitter drinks, sweet drinks, dry drinks, fruity drinks, bubbly drinks, designer drinks, and secret formula known by only three monks drinks.

And we drink drinks for lots of different reasons. To quench a thirst, or wash down a meal. For the taste, or the nose, or the bite. Sometimes to celebrate; sometimes to commiserate. To frolic; or to forget. To be in with the set; to be out with the lads. To have a good time. Or a less bad time. Or . . . anytime.

Many drinks have alcohol in them – and this is no coincidence. The advertisers wax lyrical about the sophistication of dry vermouth, the machismo of super-strong lager, the exciting bite of vodka, or the subdued sensuality of an aperitif . . . But you know and I know that what they're really talking about is that clear, colourless and almost flavourless liquid, alcohol.

Alcohol is the source of a great deal of pleasure . . . or at least the expectation of pleasure . . . and it's something that most of us enjoy, and many of us relish.

In fact, although nobody drinks alcohol as such, somehow the average person over 15 in Britain manages to pour nearly ten litres of *pure* alcohol down his or her average gullet in an average year.

Let's face it, we love the stuff! At least, I know I certainly do.

I can remember my first drink as if it was only yesterday. It was actually when I was about 14, some years ago now, and I was at a cousin's wedding. I can remember the marquee, and the flowers, and the cake. And I can remember a kindly uncle handing me what he called a 'gin and it'. I can remember him telling me it would put hairs on my chest. And that's all I can remember . . .

But I had a great time. They told me so. And I've gone on enjoying a drink ever since. Sometimes, I admit here and now, to excess. You have to be superhuman to go through university and medical school, and let's face it adult life too, without at least occasionally overdoing the alcohol.

But, of course, there's a catch. There's always a catch. There's a flip-side to alcohol. As well as being a source of so much pleasure, it can also cause an awful lot of pain. Arguments and accidents, hangovers and heartbreaks, bust-ups and beatings, slip-ups and sackings, disease, dementia and death.

As a doctor, I've seen more than a fair share of the flip-side – having spent many a night in the accident and emergency department stitching up the steady stream of 'closing-time casualties'. And having worked on the intensive care ward with dozens of patients, many quite young, at death's door with liver failure. And in general practice, having tried to help many families slowly but surely cracking up under the strain of alcohol dependence.

This is not, however, an anti-alcohol book. Instead, I hope you'll find it to be a pro-alcohol-sensibly book. I've tried to serve up a cocktail of information, anecdotes, quotes, and practical advice, in the hope that you'll not only find it interesting, but also that it may help you, and those around you, to get the very best out of drinking.

Including the best of health.

Cheers!

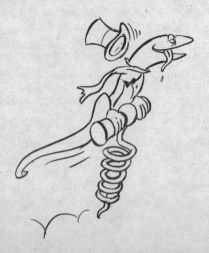

CHAPTER TWO

THE BUSINESS OF
BOOZE

Alcohol is a *huge* business. Every day, you, I, and the rest of the nation's drinkers fork out about £35 million for drink. Alcoholic drink. Yes every day.

Over 90 per cent of British adults drinks at least occasionally, and in the course of a year we currently spend about £10,000 million on beer, and getting on for another £10,000 million on wines and spirits. In doing so we provide the Chancellor with a tax rake-off of over £7 billion a year – that's £7,000,000,000 – about 5 per cent of the Government's total income, and enough to pay for roughly a third of the National Health Service.

Now there's a bizarre thought. Every third hospital bed, every third nurse, and every third doctor, are being paid for thanks to our fondness of the demon drink. How nice to know it's all going to such a good cause.

Alcohol provides plenty more direct employment too. It's reckoned that there are about 125,000 jobs in producing and marketing drink in the UK. And if you add to that all those working in our 80,000 pubs, 35,000 licensed clubs and 48,000 off-licences and other outlets, you arrive at a total of around 750,000 people. That's about one in every 30 working people in this country.

Drink also brings a great deal of money into this country from abroad. Last year we exported well over £1,000,000,000-worth of alcohol – a large proportion of which was our star product, Scotch whisky, Scotland's biggest foreign-currency earner. In fact, after France, the UK is the world's largest exporter of alcohol. True, we import a lot too – mainly wine and brandy – but the booze balance of payments is £½ million in our favour, which goes down quite well at the Department of Trade and Industry.

Many a cork is popping and glass a-clinking in the City too. Booze is certainly big business there. The major brewers have had the Stock Exchange in ferment for years, with take-overs and diversification and asset-stripping, not to mention the occasional lapse into insider-dealing.

Over the past 20 years, as the true cost of alcohol has fallen, so consumption has increased

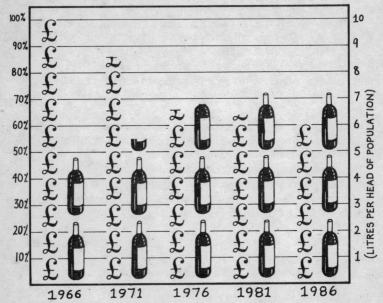

(Consumption in litres of pure alcohol per capita per annum. True cost in terms of disposable income, as a proportion of the 1966 figure)

All in all on a global scale, Oxfam has calculated that the world's drinkers spend more on their grog than it would cost to give every single man, woman and child on the planet enough food and water, adequate shelter, and good healthcare and education.

THE TRUE COST OF DRINK

But, quite apart from the money we spend on drink itself, we as a nation have to pay for the true cost of booze to our society:

- Up to a million people whose lives and health are seriously damaged by alcohol misuse.
- Over 28,000 people dying prematurely with alcohol-related illnesses every year.
- Alcohol is the main contributor to the deaths of young people – at least 1000 deaths of children and young people every year.
- Alcohol is linked to two out of three attempted suicides.
- And to one in every five general hospital admissions.
- And about 17,000 admissions to psychiatric hospitals and units every year.
- Over 120,000 people a year are convicted of drink-driving.
- Alcohol is the main contributor to deaths on the road – one quarter of all fatalities are alcohol-linked.
- And nearly half of road deaths in the under 25s.
- One in every three drivers killed is driving over the legal limit.
- Alcohol is involved in about two-thirds of head injuries.
- About one-third of domestic accidents.
- 40 per cent of fires.
- And one in five drownings.
- About 100,000 convictions a year are for drunkenness.
- And about 50 per cent of all crime is alcohol-linked.
- Drinking plays a part in about half of all murders.
- Half of all wife-batterings.
- And a high proportion of child abuse.

This is a dreadful catalogue of tragedy and misery. But in addition to the human costs, there is an economic cost too. According to Professor Alan Maynard of the Department of Health Economics, York University, the real price we pay for our drinking habit is in excess of £2,000,000,000 a year. The table overleaf shows how the sums mount up.

The Royal College of Psychiatrists sums it all up thus:

'Alcohol is the major public health issue of our time – overshadowing that of tobacco, and dwarfing the problems of illicit drug abuse.'

And yet, I almost forgot, there's one other large sum to mention . . . The drinks industry spends over £200,000,000 a year persuading us to drink *more* alcohol!

The true cost of alcohol every year

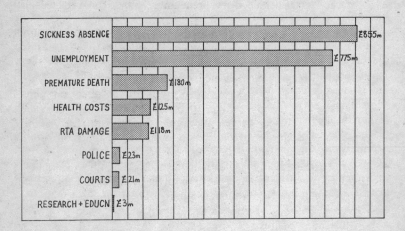

ADVERTISING

Which drink refreshes the parts other beers cannot reach? And what is 'probably the best lager in the world'? The impact of drinks advertising is such that only the strictest teetotaller, or a complete hermit, would not be able to answer at least one correctly. (The answers, for the benefit of teetotal hermits everywhere, are Heineken and Carlsberg.) Over £200 million was spent last year on extolling the virtues of booze and imprinting brand names ever more firmly on our brains. Sophisticated, sexy, comic or cool, the style and content of these adverts vary enormously, and the approach adopted for each drink will often depend on which 'target group' the advertisers are aiming at.

YOUNG PEOPLE

It might be thought that this target group is a relatively recent one, but as far back as 1933 the director of the Brewer's Society announced to a meeting in Birmingham: 'We want to get the beer-drinking habit instilled into thousands, almost millions of young men who do not at present know the taste of beer.' That year, a collective advertising campaign was launched under the banner of 'Beer is Best'. Some twenty years later, the Younger's brewery was urging Britain's four million working teenagers (with their £17 million of 'uncommitted spending power') to 'Join the Younger set. A younger taste is a taste for life.'

By 1975, the Advertising Standards Authority felt the need to introduce the Liquor Advertising Code of Practice, which included the ruling that, 'advertisements should not be directed at young people nor in any way encourage them to start drinking'. But the youth market is far too lucrative for the industry to leave alone. Indeed, some advertisers may even see the rules as a challenge to their ingenuity – how can they appeal to young people without looking as if they are? The chat show host Jonathan Ross was at the centre of controversy a couple of years ago, when he appeared in a TV advertisement for Harp lager. Despite Harp's claims that Ross was chosen for his sense of style, the ad was adjudged to contravene Rule 2 of the Independent Broadcasting Authority's own Code of Practice, which states: 'No liquor advertisement may feature any personality who commands the loyalty of the young.' The advert was consequently withdrawn from the schedules.

Although it is illegal for anyone to buy alcohol under the age of 18, it should be recognised that the audience for drink advertising extends way below that age limit. In a survey by the Association of Market Survey Organisations, twenty per cent of 13–14-year-olds chose a Carling Black Label advert as their favourite, with other beer ads also high on their lists. The message from George, the Hofmeister bear, to 'follow the bear', for example, is bound to appeal to growing youngsters who want to be cool and belong. They may not be drinking alcohol yet (though some of them are), but already the brands are known to them. An American advertising executive once said, 'Get a guy to drink your beer at college and you could get him for life'; could he also have said, 'Get a schoolkid to enjoy your ad . . .'?

'I must say I get annoyed about the beer adverts, how they're thrust down us . . . such a blur, I don't even know which one product they are advertising any more. I get drunk watching beer adverts, there's so many.'

JOHN SACHS

WOMEN

> *'The most beautiful drink in the world. Whenever beautiful girls get together Babycham is the first choice – for its gay, sparkling personality.'*

Glamour, beauty and social success were all promised to young women in this ad from the 1960s, and these enticements are as strong as ever today. However, the advertising now aimed at women is far broader in its scope. With increased spending power and access to more and more drink in shops, women are regarded as the most exploitable group of alcohol consumers. Here is a real 'growth market'. Some adverts ooze with sophistication and sensuality, attempting to persuade women that life is somehow empty or unfulfilled or just plain dull without this or that brand of aperitif, vermouth or vodka. Others present the rising numbers of working women with a more individual image, offering independence but still, of course, desirability. With a vast choice of drinks widely available on supermarket shelves, it has never been easier for women to respond to the pressures of advertising and take home a clinking basket of dreams – whether to re-create a sultry Caribbean beach on the back patio, or a chic New York soiree in the sitting room.

> *'When he asks you "What's yours?", say SKOL and enjoy this superb Dry Lager that's right in fashion.'*
> Lager ad from a 1950s women's magazine

The modern woman needn't wait for a man to ask her what she wants to drink – she buys her own. With beer sales to men at saturation point, we are now seeing new lager brands targeted specifically at women – usually premium lager in smart, foil-wrapped bottles, such as Bleu de Brasserie, the first tailor-made tipple for the younger independent woman.

'Any time, any place, anywhere . . .' Martini and Cinzano have always been aimed primarily at the female market, the latter to the slightly older and more sophisticated woman. But now both are concentrating their efforts at the younger end of the age-range. So, too, are the new breed of 'instant cocktail' drinks, such as Bezique and Taboo. And the advertisers' efforts are being rewarded. Young women are flocking into the new brasserie and cocktail-bar-style pubs, wine-bars and disco-clubs. No longer dependent on men for company or cash, they are ordering whatever takes their fancy. And the market continues to grow.

HEAVY DRINKERS

TV images of sweat, muscle, and the shining steel of heavy industry, backed by the song 'It's a man's, man's world'. No, it's not an ad for Babycham! The advertisers for Tennants Extra Strong lager know their target audience. It needn't bother them if some viewers look upon the macho values respresented as outdated, risible or offensive. Since a macho outlook readily accepts the ritual of heavy drinking, the ad is most likely to strike a chord in men who spend above-average amounts of money on alcohol. That's fine with the brewers.

Risk-taking and reckless behaviour are prominent amongst alcoholics and heavy drinkers. Adverts that may appeal to such personalities are, to an extent, curbed by Rule 11 of the IBA's Liquor Advertising Code of Practice, which states that, 'Treatments featuring special daring or toughness must not be used in a way which is likely to associate the act of drinking with masculinity.' A complaint was recently upheld by the Advertising Standards Authority against an ad which showed a man with a surfboard pouring a glass of Newcastle Brown Ale, with the caption: 'Keep a Cool Head'. The ASA agreed with the London Alcohol Policy Group (which had lodged the complaint) that it was misleading to suggest that one could remain sober and in command after drinking alcohol, and the advertisers were advised to 'adopt an alternative approach in future'.

'CONNOISSEURS'

Flattery will get you everywhere. There are plenty of adverts which try to convince the consumer that if he or she is a person of taste, they will buy the product concerned. Ads for liqueurs and fortified wines, such as sherry and port, tend to accentuate class and a discerning palate. Some beers also adopt this approach. 'Probably the best lager in the world' is a case in point.

The advertisers of Guinness are conscious that its distinctive taste makes it more marketable to people who see themselves as individuals and not susceptible to the herd instinct. Their latest TV campaign, featuring actor Rutger Hauer as a cool Martian with a surrealist view of life on Earth, is aimed specifically at this target group, or herd of individuals!

UNDER THE INFLUENCE OF ADVERTISING? ....

In 1987, the Masham Report on young people and alcohol concluded: 'Given the scale of the problems caused by alcohol abuse, cinema and TV advertising of all alcoholic groups should be banned.' Naturally, the advertisers and the drinks industry disagree. The purpose of advertising, they maintain, is to boost sales of one particular brand at the expense of others, rather than boost sales of alcohol overall. In their defence, they point out that alcohol consumption has remained at a reasonably steady level, despite hefty increases in spending on advertising. What they don't ask, though, is how much consumption might have fallen if that money hadn't been spent.

The Advertising Association has produced its own report in response to Masham, claiming that advertising has little or no effect on young people's drinking and is popular only for its entertainment value. It is certainly fair to draw a distinction between ads that entertain and those that actually sell. Since their early campaigns in the 1930s ('My goodness – my Guinness'), Guinness adverts have enjoyed a good reputation. However, as one of their advertising managers made clear twenty years ago, entertainment is not their primary goal: 'Some people used to adore the ads, but never drank the stuff. Those were great days, but times have changed.' Similarly, in 1983, a hugely popular series of half-minute sketches featuring Joan Collins and Leonard Rossiter was dropped by Cinzano executives, who felt that the regular spillage of their precious product over Ms Collins' dresses was doing nothing for the drink's image, or sales.

....

'The notion that drinks advertising only causes brand switching is nonsense. If you look at the specialist journals for marketing executives, you will see a lot of discussion of the untapped market of women drinkers, for instance, and efforts are discussed of how on earth we are going to get them to drink more ... Now, the notion that maleness and masculinity is associated with drinking alcohol is not a new one, it's been around for thousands of years, but the notion that feminine sexuality is associated with drinking is a very new one that is quite a dangerous creation of the drinks industry.'

Dr Ian Robertson

....

Whilst accepting it was difficult to prove that advertising increased consumption, the Masham Report did feel that 'the nature of advertising helped to create the climate in which alcohol is seen as an indispensable adjunct to almost all social occasions'. The Campaign for Real Ale, though looking at the problem from a slightly different angle, has also called for a ban on adverts which give alcohol a glamorous or trendy image; this is part of their charter to 'restore the British pub to its rightful place at the heart of our social lives, and to encourage sensible drinking'.

It is very easy to blame Britain's alcohol-related problems on advertising. But, as the president of the Distilled Spirits Council in the USA once said: 'There was no advertising during Prohibition.' Nor were there any TV drink ads during this country's gin epidemic in the eighteenth century! It needs to be remembered that there are other cultural, psychological and political factors which determine a nation's drinking habits. Higher taxation on alcoholic drinks is the single most likely key to a decline in our overall consumption. However, in its work for the drinks industry and as part of our culture, advertising also plays its part. Even if it *could* be proved that adverts for alcoholic drinks do nothing to increase our consumption, no one would argue that they encourage us to cut down!

GREAT (ALCOHOLIC) MOMENTS IN HISTORY

For all we know, the dinosaurs were drunkards and Australopithecus was pithed for most of his miserable life. However, our first real inkling of the part that alcohol has played in history comes from a few fragments of clay, dug up from the ruins of ancient Babylon. These fragile tablets suggest that beer was being drunk as long ago as 5000 BC. Mesopotamian wine goblets have also been found dating back to 3000 BC, although it is thought that wine was probably discovered before beer. According to the Bible, Noah planted the very first vineyard after the Flood.

'And Noah began to be an husbandman, and he planted a vineyard; and he drank of the wine, and was drunken; and was uncovered within his tent.'

Genesis 9: 20–21

If grapes are left to decay naturally, it takes only a small amount of airborne yeast to start the fermentation process. So, like many great discoveries, it was probably by accident that wine was first made and tasted. One story tells of the Persian King Jamshid who, in order to enjoy eating grapes all the year round, kept a large supply in reserve down in his cellars. He also, it appears, kept plenty of lovers in reserve. One particular favourite, when replaced by the next pretty member of his harem, was so distressed that she resolved to kill herself. Her choice of poison was the juice of rotten grapes from the foulest-smelling jar in the Palace. The court was understandably amazed when the jilted lover, tearful only hours before, reappeared from the cellars with flushed cheeks and a curiously happy smile on her face. The king was so struck by her radiance that he fell for her all over again. This may well have been the first time anyone asked 'What's your poison?'

*'Give me eighteen bowls of wine. Behold, I love
drunkenness.'*

Egyptian female courtier
(17th Dynasty hieroglyphics)

No one knows for sure when the first spirits were distilled, though the Chinese are thought to have been drinking a raw kind of rice spirit by about 1000 BC. The Latin term for spirits was *aqua vitae*, meaning 'the water of life'. Translated into old Celtic it becomes *uisge beatha* – and it's from this expression that the word 'whisky' is derived. Likewise, the Russian for 'water of life' is *zhizennia voda*, more fondly known as 'vodka'. While we're at it, the word 'alcohol' comes from Arabic – *al* means 'the', and *kohl* is the fine powder of antimony (a brittle, bluish white metal), which is used in the East as a cosmetic on the eyelids. *Al kohl* came to mean 'essence', and hence was used to describe the distillate of fermented grapes – referred to by the French as *alcool* and by the more guttural English as 'alcohol'.

Alexander the Great would have lived longer than his 33 years if he'd gone a bit easier on the booze. (So would a friend of his, whom he killed in a drunken brawl.) On his last binge, he drank to the health of 20 guests, each one in turn, repeated the act, and then called for 'the cup of Hercules', which contained six bottles worth of wine. He downed two of these before collapsing on to the the floor. Carried to his bed, he soon developed a fever and, shortly afterwards, died.

The Romans, keen wine-drinkers, planted vines wherever they conquered, but we know that the Britons drank wine before they arrived, as wine storage jars have been found in pre-Roman burial chambers. Whereas the Britons drank their wine neat, the Romans tended to mix theirs with water, which may explain why their roads were straighter.

One tradition the Romans did leave us was the building of *tavernae* (taverns) by the roads. It was they, too, who gave us our first taste of bitter, by importing hops from the continent. It didn't catch on first time round though – we reverted to unhopped ale as soon as the Romans left.

*'The decay of man and manliness led to the fall of the
Roman Empire, and this decay was due, in a large
measure, to the influence of Bacchus (God of Wine).'*
Temperance History, DAWSON BURNS

The next conquerors of Britain, the Vikings, drank ale and cider, rather than wine, and downing a hornful (about a litre) in one go was a common practice. The Normans, in turn, preferred wine. But one thing they all had in common, whether Roman, Briton, Viking or Norman: whatever they drank, they drank a lot.

In monasteries, wine was used both for sacramental purposes and for refreshment. Monks used to taste the soil before deciding where to plant their vines, and in some cases this may even have dictated the siting of the monasteries themselves. British wine production, however, which had always been a battle due to the soil and climate, declined rapidly after 1152, when Prince Henry (later King Henry II) married Eleanor of Aquitaine, whose dowry included the top wine-producing regions of Normandy, Brittany, Anjou and Gascony. For the next 300 years Bordeaux was an everyday English drink.

'A soldier must not get drunk more often than once a week. It would, of course, be better if he did not get drunk at all, but one should not expect the impossible.'

GENGHIS KHAN 1162–1227

Our forefathers were just as concerned about the size of their drinks as we are today, and the Magna Carta (1215) included a statement on standard measures for ale and wine. And in 1267 the Assize of Bread and Ale heralded an attempt to exercise control over the price and quality of ale produced. Special inspectors, called 'conners', would call on ale houses to test the strength of their brews. Legend has it that they always wore leather breeches, and carried out the test by pouring some of the ale on to a wooden bench and then sitting on it. If the bench failed to stick to their backsides when they rose, the ale was reckoned to be understrength.

Hops made their brewing comeback in the fifteenth century, though it took a while for the British to get used to the 'bitter' taste. Bitter's initial lack of popularity was reflected in its price – half that of ale – but by the early 1700s we had acquired the taste and the first large breweries were founded. Making full use of James Watt's recent advances with steam, they soon brought an end to the days when every farmer made his own 'home brew'. By the nineteenth century beer was especially popular, as it was safer to drink than water, which was usually polluted, and cheaper than tea, coffee or cocoa.

Examples of strong ales during the reign of Elizabeth I (1558–1603) included 'dagger ale', 'doble-doble', 'dragon's milk' and 'merry-go-round'.

In the 1580s, English soldiers who were helping the Dutch in their revolt against the Spanish (in what were then the Spanish Netherlands) drowned their sorrows and their fears by drinking raw spirits before going into battle. This they called 'Dutch courage'.

In the 1660s, with Cromwell in command and Puritanism a dominant force, a common punishment for drunkenness was the 'Drunkard's Cloak'. This was a large barrel, with holes cut in for the head and legs, worn by the offender as he was marched along the public streets.

> *'Under the Cathedral-church at Hereford is the greatest Charnelhouse for bones, that ever I saw in England . . . Cunning alewives putt the Ashes of these bones in their Ale to make it intoxicateing.'*
> JOHN AUBREY 1626–97

Ten years earlier, in 1650, Franciscus Sylvius (also known as Franciscus de la Boe), a professor of medicine at the University of Leyden (Holland), distilled a quantity of fermented barley but found the resultant liquid's taste so disgusting that he added juniper berries. This was far more pleasing to the palate, and it has pleased many palates since. The dutch word for juniper is *genever*, which the English language soon distilled to 'gin'.

Gin was widely drunk in Britain after the Dutch King William III came to the throne in 1689, but its consumption increased alarmingly from the beginning of the eighteenth century. When wealthy landowners found themselves with a grain surplus, the Government came to their assistance and encouraged the distilling of gin from grain by loosening the licensing laws. With no licence required to sell it, the national figures for gin consumption rose from half a million gallons in 1700 to more than 5 million gallons in 1735. Gin shops sprang up everywhere – a typical pub-sign of the times offered: 'Drunk for 1d. Dead drunk for 2d. Clean straw for nothing.' Drunkards littered the streets of London and thousands of addicts followed the downward path of pawning, robbery and murder to assuage their thirst for 'the great destroyer'. Mothers even gave gin to their babies to make them sleep. With the 1736 Gin Act the Government attempted to raise the price of gin above the means of the poor, but shops sidestepped the legislation by calling their spirits different names, such as 'Grape Waters', 'Ladies' Delight' and 'Cuckold's Comfort' – anything, in fact, but gin. Between 1740 and 1742, when the gin epidemic was at its height, there were twice as many burials in London as christenings. In 1751, Parliament tried again, introducing severe penalties for illegal distilling, more limits on the retail price of spirits, and a far heavier tax. The Great British public responded with riots but, with the poor turning reluctantly back to beer, annual gin consumption was down to one million gallons by 1800 from a peak of 8 million gallons.

Madeira (wine fortified with brandy), from the Portuguese island of the same name, became popular in England after the marriage of Charles II and Catherine of Braganza, a Portuguese princess, in 1661. Up until Victorian times, a glass of Madeira and a slice of Madeira cake made for a popular morning refreshment amongst well-to-do ladies.

Admiral Vernon was not a popular figure with sailors when, in 1740, he decided that their rum ration should be watered down. He was already known as 'old grog' due to the grogram cloak he wore, grogram being a coarse cloth made from silk and wool. The name 'grog' lived on after him, to describe any mixture of spirits and water.

- -

William Pitt the Younger (1759–1806) once allegedly drank 574 bottles of claret, 854 bottles of Madeira and 2410 bottles of Port in one year. This works out to a daily average of 1.57 bottles of claret, 2.33 of Madeira, and 6.6 of Port!

- -

In the eighteenth century it was common for the gentry to spend the evening drinking themselves into a stupor. Often there would be a butler or two standing by the dining-room door with a barrow, ready to cart those who had passed out off to their beds. The average, less well-off member of the public could only dream about that sort of service when *he* got 'drunk as a lord'.

At a packed temperance meeting in September 1833, a reformed drunkard called Dicky Turner brought a new word into the English language. There was at that time a split in the anti-drinking lobby between the Moderationists and the Total Abstainers. An eager speaker for the latter, and with a flair for the dramatic, Dicky Turner declared: 'Nothing

Three hundred years of alcohol consumption

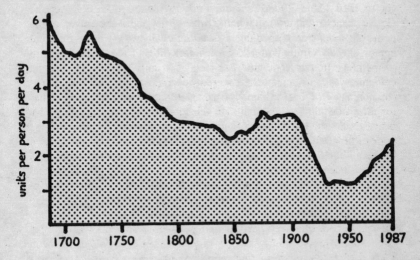

Source: Adapted from Spring and Buss, Nature, 15 Dec 1977

but the T-T-Total will do!' From that evening on, the abstainers were known as 'teetotallers'.

> *The Saloon Bar: a bar to Heaven, a door to Hell –*
> *Whoever named it, named it well!*
> Words of a temperance writer near the turn of the
> century.

The most vigorous campaigner for Prohibition, however, was probably a certain Ms Carry Nation, member of the Women's Christian Temperance Union, who, in between choruses of 'Onward Christian Soldiers', 'No Hope for the Drunkard' and other temperance classics, chopped up bars and saloons with a hatchet.

In 1897, Britain's first convicted drunken driver was fined a pound for being drunk in charge of his electrically-powered taxi.

Explorers of the Nile lived on flesh of crocodile,
yet as they mapped their tracks throughout the jungle,
they never died of ague or some other beastly plague.
With a Scotch aboard, a bwana couldn't stumble.
Good show!
Bung ho!
Sad the British Empire took a tumble.
Some think
strong drink
caused the mighty British Raj to bungle.
But in battle's heat we showed a double scotch and
soda
fanned the flames and gave us bags of fire.
With soda or with water, just a dash, and into
slaughter.
We helped build the British Empire.

PETER CHRISTIE

In the First World War, drink was seen as a genuine threat to Britain's security. Soldiers' send-offs were invariably drunken occasions, and soon the face of the Secretary of State for War looked out from posters declaring: 'Lord Kitchener appeals to everyone: Avoid Treating the Men to Drink.' The civilian population was also turning to the bottle. As one government minister remarked: 'We are fighting Germany, Austria and the drink, and as far as I can see, the greatest of these deadly foes is drink.' To counter this 'deadly foe', opening hours were considerably restricted and alcohol was subjected to a string of tax increases. The strength of beer was also reduced, the weaker brews coming to be known, disparagingly, as 'government ale'.

In January 1920, The Eighteenth Amendment introduced Prohibition to the USA, a ban on alcohol which resulted in previously moderate Americans doing all they could to get hold of a drink, much to the delight of racketeers like Al Capone. Here the cocktail was born, as imaginative bartenders mixed in other drinks to cover the biting taste of illicitly distilled 'bath-tub gin'. Prohibition ended 13 years later, under the newly-elected Franklin D. Roosevelt, who had promised 'a New Deal and a pot of beer for everyone'.

'I was T T until Prohibition!'

GROUCHO MARX

The world's first can of beer came onto the market in 1935, a US brew called Krueger.

The world's first breathalyser, known as the 'Drunkometer', was used by US police on New Year's Eve, 1938.

The Second World War brought about very little in the way of a change in Britain's drinking habits, but the 1950s, 1960s and 1970s saw a marked rise in home drinking, prompted by the proliferation of refrigerators, television sets and the sale of low-price alcohol in supermarkets and off-licences. The emancipation of women and the increased spending power of that new form of being, 'the teenager', saw an expansion both in the women's and youth markets.

In the 1980s, Britain has gained a certain notoriety for its drinking habits abroad. With 'lager louts' revelling in the low prices of drink when on holiday in Spain, it's odd to note that the package tour industry owes its beginnings to a complete abstainer. Thomas Cook, founder of the world famous travel agency, first learnt about organising cheap travel for the many in 1841, when he arranged for a special train to take 570 people from Leicester to a temperance meeting in Loughborough. Some years later, on a tour of Italy, some members of the party were about to buy a drop or two of cheap local wine. Thomas Cook called after them: 'Gentlemen, do not invest your money in diarrhoea!'

The average price of a pint of draught bitter was...

76p in 1987
40p in 1980
10p in 1970
1p in 1912

and less than ½p in 1847!

On 22 August 1988, Britain's new licensing law came into effect, allowing landlords to keep their premises open all afternoon if they so wished. Would the result be an increase in drunkenness, or a more measured approach to drinking? Supporters of both arguments have already produced figures to back up their claims.

Aquarius, a Birmingham-based alcohol counselling service, made a comparison of the number of appearances at a local court for alcohol-related offences before and after the change in the law. The crime figures for the month after 22 August showed an increase of 23.6 per cent on the previous month. The increase for those two months in 1987 had been just 6 per cent, leading the study to conclude that the change in the law had indeed had a detrimental effect on drinking habits.

On the other hand, the man responsible for the new law, Home Secretary Douglas Hurd, quoted police figures for 'one of the toughest parts of London' where arrests for drunkenness had dropped by 25 per cent in the four weeks following the change in the law.

So, the statistical battle has started. However, it will probably be years rather than months before a reliable pattern emerges.

KNOW YOUR LIMITS

> *'Abstinence is a good thing – but it should always be practised in moderation.'*
>
> Anon

Of course, it's up to you what you drink, when you drink, and how much you drink. There are restrictions on the age at which you can drink, for obvious and very good reasons (*see* p.95). And there are designated hours for pub drinking. But broadly speaking, compared with many other countries in the world, or states in the USA, Britain has a liberal attitude to alcohol, and the individual has a pretty free hand. It's up to each and every one of us to decide whether we open that can of beer, pour that glass of wine, order that round of drinks, or put that extra bottle of sherry in the shopping basket.

And most of us face these decisions many times a week. True, the price of drink makes a big difference as to how often we might be tempted. And, of course, the more often we're faced with the opportunity to buy or pour a drink, the more decisions we have to make.

But what are the sensible limits? How do we know how much we can drink, on a week-by-week basis, without doing ourselves any long-term harm? I'm not talking here about how much we can drink without going over the legal limit for driving. That's another issue, and I will go into that in some depth in Chapter 12.

No, I'm looking at the level of drinking our body and soul can handle over a period of time without running into the many and various hazards to health that I describe in Chapter 8.

Well, as you can imagine, the question of sensible and 'safe' limits has been thoroughly investigated by the health experts in this, and many other countries. And although it's actually not an easy question to answer, because alcohol affects the body in so many different ways, you'll be pleased to know that they have arrived at some simple clear guidelines.

'They', by the way, are the Royal College of Physicians, the Royal College of Psychiatrists, the Royal College of General Practitioners, the Health Education Authority for England, the Scottish Health Education Group, the Welsh Health Promotion Authority, the Government Health Departments, and a number of other key organisations concerned with alcohol and its effects.

'Your average British man likes to go and have a pint in the pub and enjoy it, and it's an intelligent man who can go there and know his limits.'

GRAEME SOUNESS

EACH DRINK EQUALS 1 UNIT

| ½ pint of ordinary lager, beer or cider | ¼ pint of strong lager, beer or cider | 1 small glass of table wine | 1 single pub measure of spirits | 1 small glass of sherry or port |

'A STANDARD UNIT PLEASE, ... WITH ICE AND LEMON'

By an amazing piece of good fortune, and a little bit of wishful thinking, certain standard measures of the most popular drinks all happen to have roughly the same amount of alcohol in them. Incredible, but more or less true.

It just so happens that a half-pint of ordinary bitter, lager or cider; a pub glass of wine; a pub schooner of sherry, port or vermouth; or a single pub measure of spirits, each contain about 8–10 grams of alcohol. So, each of these items can be regarded as one standard unit or standard drink.

It's all so beautifully simple! Of course, it's a bit too simple. Even though they shouldn't, pub measures of wine and fortified wines like sherry and port do vary quite a bit. Even a single spirit measure differs whether you're in England and Wales (1/6 gill), Scotland (1/5 gill) or Ireland (1/4 gill). At least a pint is a pint is a pint. Needless to say, home measures of almost anything are infinitely more generous. And as the table on p.38 shows, there's a wide range of alcoholic strengths among beers and wines particularly.

Nevertheless, bearing in mind all these provisos, the standard unit of alcohol (usually abbreviated to 'unit') is a handy concept, and is a great help in giving us a rough idea of how much alcohol we're taking on board and what level it's likely to reach in our bloodstream.

THE SENSIBLE LIMIT

The limit depends on sex. For the reasons I will go into in Chapter 9, women are more susceptible to the long-term effects of alcohol, they have a lower margin of safety, and therefore it's sensible for them to drink less.

FOR MEN

the sensible limit is up to 21 units a week, spread throughout the week, so that there are two or three days completely without alcohol.

So, for instance, two or three pints of ordinary beer, lager or cider, two or three times a week, would be fine, with a few units to spare – *as long as you're not driving (or operating machinery)*. Remember that three pints (six units) is likely to take you over the legal limit for driving.

FOR WOMEN

the sensible limit is up to 14 units a week, spread throughout the week, so that there are two or three days completely without alcohol.

So, for instance, two or three glasses of wine, three or four times a week, would be comfortably within the limit – *as long as you're not pregnant (see p.88). And remember that, for some smaller, slimmer women, even three glasses of wine can reach the legal limit for driving.*

But leaving the immediate effects aside, from the point of view of long-term health, drinking within your sensible limit is perfectly safe. Think of it as a 'green light'. Going a little above the level sometimes, into the 'amber', is unlikely to do any harm – as long as it is only sometimes, because the risks do begin to creep up.

THE WARNING ZONE

FOR MEN
drinking more than 35 units a week is increasingly likely to do long-term harm.

FOR WOMEN
drinking more than 21 units a week is increasingly likely to do long-term harm.

Above this level, you're into the red-for-warning zone, and you're drinking too much. In this zone, risks to your health rise steeply the more you drink. Remember these warning levels are for people of average height and build for their sex. Smaller, slimmer people risk running into trouble at lower levels than these. For details of the sort of trouble, see Chapter 8.

THE DANGER ZONE

FOR MEN
More than 50 units a week is definitely damaging.

FOR WOMEN
More than 35 units a week is definitely damaging.

At this level the situation is potentially serious, and it's very important for your health's sake to cut down. The liver damage alone is worrying enough, without going into all the other problems that you're pouring down your throat. It may not seem much to you – for a man, say, a pint at lunchtime and two or three of an evening; or for a woman, perhaps, a glass or two of wine at lunchtime and three or four of an evening. But day in day out, week in week out, year in year out, it takes its toll. What may be small beer in your book, is very heavy drinking for your liver, your brain, your heart and circulation, and quite probably your job, your bank balance and your love life. Very heavy drinking is sooner or later problem drinking, and you may need help (*see* Chapter 13).

   Talking of heavy, I'm sorry if all this comes across as a bit too heavy. But I think it has to be. Because it really is the crunchpoint in dealing with drink. If you're one of the 6 per cent of men, or 1 per cent of women in the danger zone (multiply those rates by two for 18–35-year-olds), and these words manage to persuade you to do something about cutting down then I think it would have been worth all the weight I've given it.

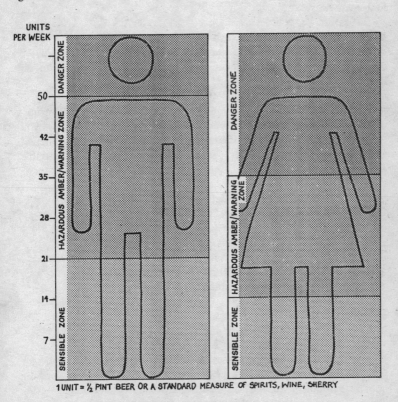

UNITS PER WEEK

DANGER ZONE

HAZARDOUS AMBER/WARNING ZONE

SENSIBLE ZONE

50
42
35
28
21
14
7

DANGER ZONE

HAZARDOUS AMBER/WARNING ZONE

SENSIBLE ZONE

1 UNIT = ½ PINT BEER OR A STANDARD MEASURE OF SPIRITS, WINE, SHERRY

GRADUALLY INCREASING RISK

With these limits, levels and zones, it's important to remember that they aren't hard lines etched into tablets of stone. You don't suddenly flip from the warning zone into the danger zone with just one extra drink a week. Life isn't quite like that. As with so many other things which bear on our health, there is a gradual increase in risk as the dose gets higher – from virtually negligible risk in the sensible zone, to slightly higher risks as you go up through the amber zone, merging into more and more significant risks through the warning zone, and becoming ever-increasing harm in the danger zone.

SENSIBLE ZONE

| Men: | 1–21 units/week | Light drinking. |
| Women: | 1–14 units/week | Safest for health. |

AMBER ZONE

| Men: | 22–35 units/week | Moderate drinking. |
| Women: | 15–21 units/week | Harm unlikely, but take care. |

WARNING ZONE

| Men: | 36–50 units/week | Fairly heavy drinking. Harm to |
| Women: | 22–35 units/week | health is likely. |

DANGER ZONE

| Men: | 51+ units/week | Very heavy drinking. Definitely |
| Women: | 36+ units/week | damaging to health. |

Investigators at King's College School of Medicine recently sent a questionnaire to 1500 employees of a large London company, from the shop floor to the boardroom, asking them about their drinking habits. They found that about one in three men, and one in five women, were regularly drinking more than the recommended sensible limits (up to 21 units a week for men, and 14 units a week for women).

What's more, one in ten of both sexes were exceeding higher levels likely to damage their health (more than 35 units for men, and 21 units for women).

About 75 per cent of those surveyed felt it

would be quite acceptable to consume half a
bottle of wine or two pints of beer every
lunchtime. Many reckoned that turning up for
work with a hangover was all par for the course.
And, when asked what they'd do if alcohol was
unavailable, a full 22 per cent said they would
brew or ferment their own.

HOW MUCH DO YOU *REALLY* DRINK?

But, knowing what the limits are is no good if you have no idea what you
are *really* drinking. Many of us reckon we've got a pretty good idea, but
often this bears no relation to reality.

Perhaps we've got a vague notion that we 'like a few beers of an
evening', or 'do rather enjoy the odd glass of wine', or 'never say no to a
little liquid hospitality'. But if really pressed on precisely what we've
consumed in the way of alcohol over the past week, how many of us can
really put our hand on our heart and say we really have got an accurate
account of it?

If you're someone who has a drink most days of the week, it's both
an interesting and informative exercise to try to think back and tot up the
tots. You might even surprise yourself, especially if you do it properly and
work out how many units of alcohol your drinking amounts to.
Remember:

> 1 *half* of ordinary bitter, lager or cider
> 1 *quarter* pint of strong bitter, lager or cider
> 1 pub glass of table wine
> 1 *single* pub measure of whisky, gin, vodka, brandy or rum
> 1 *small* pub schooner of sherry or port
> 1 pub glass of vermouth

. . . are each one unit of alcohol. And the following are rather more . . .

> 1 *can* of ordinary beer or lager = 1½ units
> 1 *bottle* of super, special or extra-strong lager = 2½ units
> 1 *can* of strong cider = 3 units
> 1 *can* of super, special or extra-strong lager = 4 units

1 *bottle* (75cl) of table wine = 7 units
1 *litre* bottle of table wine = 10 units

And if you're into serious drinking . . .

1 *bottle* of sherry, port, vermouth = 14 units
1 *bottle* of spirits = 30 units

COMPILING A DRINK DIARY

Armed with this checklist, construct for yourself a 'Drink Diary' for the past seven days (or if this wasn't a very typical week's drinking for you, then pick a week that was). For each day, have a column for the day, time, place, who with, what doing, or how feeling, and how many units. If you can't even begin to remember this for yesterday, let alone this time last week, then I suggest you start filling in the diary from this moment on, for the next week.

Here's the start of a chart to show you the sort of thing I mean:

PETER'S DRINKING DIARY

Day	Time	Place	Who with	What doing	How feeling	Drinks	Units
Monday	1-2	Badger's Wine Bar	Judith	eating	relaxed	Wine (3 glasses)	3
	5.30-7.80	Hope & Anchor	Nigel & Barry	talking shop	a bit tired	lager (3 pints)	6
Tuesday	1-2	The Sun	Richard B.	eating & discussing deal	alert	lager (1½ pints)	3
	9.30-11.80	The Goat	the lads	darts	great	bitter (4 pints)	8

Just a couple of points to bear in mind as you fill up the chart . . .

●   Be honest with yourself. There's absolutely no point in 'giving yourself the benefit of the doubt' and underestimating your intake. That makes the whole exercise a waste of time.
●   Remember that home measures are usually larger than pub measures – quite a bit larger! At home you probably only get about six glasses out of a 75cl wine bottle, compared to a pub's seven. I'll bet your sherries are a lot larger too. And let's face it, it's awfully easy to forget to stop pouring gin or whisky. Do your best to estimate the true equivalent in pub terms.

At the end of the week, add up your units to get a grand total. You may be surprised how grand it is! Then compare this with the *recommended sensible limits* for the 'average' man and woman (see p.22). Anything over these limits, and you're beginning to build up some risk of developing a problem with drink. The more units you're taking on board, the more potentially hazardous is your drinking, and the more likely you are to run into trouble – perhaps literally.

WHAT'S IN YOUR
DRINK?

A cherry?
Ice and lemon?
A dash of tabasco?
Two and a half drops of angostura?

Some of us can be ultra pernickerty about what we like in our drink to give it that something extra special. But how often do we actually think about what's *really* in the drink itself?

You may say, what does it matter as long as it looks good, tastes good and doesn't knock your head off? Fair enough. But then, when you consider that the average person over 15 sips their way through nearly 150 litres of assorted alcoholic drinks in the course of a year, it seems only reasonable to stop and think for a moment about what exactly we are pouring down our throats.

A FEW BASIC INGREDIENTS

WATER ....

The main ingredient, needless to say, is water. It provides the bulk of the drink in all but a few of the strongest liqueurs and aquavits, such as cana, a spirit distilled in Majorca, which is a mere 25 per cent water. So-called 'neat' spirits in Britain are about 60 per cent water by volume.

The water comes from a wide variety of sources. The traditional heartland of English brewing was centred on the aquifers feeding the Trent. A certain well-known Irish stout was said to lift its water from the tributaries of the Liffey. The Scots speak fondly of the peat-flavoured burns that are reputed to lend a hint of the Highlands to their whisky. The wine-makers of Bordeaux, Burgundy and Bulgaria, however, get theirs from the grapes.

'Water in moderation cannot hurt anybody.'
MARK TWAIN

So, depending on the drink being made, and the process used in making it – whether it's brewing malted barley, fermenting grapejuice or distilling spirit – different amounts of water may or may not be added or taken away. But, in all cases, water is an important ingredient in the final product.

SUGARS AND OTHER SUBSTANCES

Sugars – such as glucose and fructose in grapes, or glucose and maltose in malted barley – are a necessary part of every alcoholic drink – at least in the early stages of its manufacture, if not in the end result. Alcohol is made by the fermentation of sugars, and in all but the driest of drinks some sugars are left unfermented to make the mixture palatable. Only neat spirits are as near as dammit sugar-free. Dry wines are about 0.5 per cent sugar; medium-dry about 3 per cent; and sweet about 6 per cent. Beers and lagers vary around the 2–4 per cent mark – even draught bitter is 1½ or 2 per cent sugar. Cream sherry is about 7 per cent. Port about 12 per cent. Sweet vermouth 16 per cent. And most liqueurs are as high as 30 per cent – that's one-third sugar.

Then there are a great many other organic and inorganic substances, some present only in tiny amounts, that give a drink its subtleties of flavour, colour, texture and mystery. Some are organic acids, such as tartaric acid in wines, and malic acid in ciders. Some are aromatic esters, imparting a fruitiness. Some are tannins, giving a bitterness. All play their part in making one drink different from another. These assorted organic chemicals are called, in the trade, 'congeners', and whilst they are present in negligible quantities in some drinks, notably vodka, they can contribute nearly 3 per cent of the total ingredients of others, such as bourbon. What's more, it's now known that congeners, along with alcohol, also play a part in giving us hangovers (*see* Chapter 15). As well as these organic substances, however, there may be others of some nutritional value, notably vitamins of the B complex in beers and stouts, and a variety of inorganic substances, such as the high iron content of some wines.

... AND LAST BUT NOT LEAST ... ALCOHOL

Yes, of course, alcohol. Or really, to be technically correct, alcohols – because there's a whole family of them, many highly toxic. And several can be present in any particular drink – although, I hasten to add, in only tiny quantities, apart from one particular and very important alcohol. That one is ethyl alcohol – or ethanol. C_2H_5OH – and whenever I refer to 'alcohol' in this book, I'm talking about ethyl alcohol.

In its pure form it's a colourless, inflammable liquid, with a slight but characteristic smell, and a strong burning taste that would tear the top layer off your tongue if you were mad enough to try it. It's used as an industrial solvent, cleaning agent and fuel – and is often adulterated with its foul-tasting poisonous cousin, methyl alcohol, in methylated spirit ('meths'), in order to prevent its misuse by making it undrinkable. Skid-row drinkers, who may be tempted to pour a little meths in their strong cider, will soon end up demented and blinded by it.

Alcohol is produced by the action of yeasts – fungi which feed on sugars, making alcohol and the gas, carbon dioxide, as by-products. This is the chemical process of 'fermentation', a form of rotting, and it carries on until all the sugar is used up, or until the alcohol builds up to a level which kills off the yeast (about 14 per cent), or until the brewer/wine-maker decides that enough is enough. The carbon dioxide, incidentally, is what gives beer its head and champagne its sparkle.

BEER

The sugars used to make beer are derived from barley grain which has been allowed to germinate. This sweetens it, turning it into malt, which is then dried, roasted to give it colour and flavour, stirred into warm water to form a sugary mash called wort, mixed with hops to add a bitter flavour, and finally brewed with yeast to make beer.

Traditionally, British beer is top-brewed – the yeast floats on the top of the brew – and the resulting beer is strictly speaking an 'ale'. Most of the rest of the world drinks beer that is bottom-brewed – like lager. The word 'beer' is simply the generic for all barley brews.

Each of these two methods uses a different strain of brewer's yeast – saccharomyces ('sugar-fungus') – giving each type of beer a different aromatic flavour. The degree of bitterness is determined by the amount of 'hopping' – so bitter has more hops than mild. Colour differences are achieved by different degrees of roasting the malt – so stouts are more deeply roasted than pale ales. And the alcoholic strength is fixed by the length of time the beer is left brewing – 'winter warmers' brew longer than light ales. So-called 'barley wines' are very strong brews. Pils (or pilsener) is simply a rather superior and stronger lager. And 'diet pils' (or more correctly 'diat-pils') is a pils that has brewed nearly all the sugar out, and is therefore even stronger than ordinary pils (but because it has more alcohol, is still high in calories – so dieters beware!).

The alcoholic strength of the average British pint has fallen from around 5½ per cent at the turn of the century to less than 4 per cent today.

Extra strong lagers are nearly three times as strong as ordinary beers and lagers.

WINE

The sugars used to make wine are present in ripened grapes – some more ripened than others, depending on the climate. Northern hocks are usually lighter in alcohol because the grapejuice has relatively little sugar in it. By contrast, Mediterranean wines are full and heavy; the high alcohol content coming from the sun-drenched, well-ripened, sugary grapes. For those grapes at the cooler end of the climatic scale, extra sugar has to be added during fermentation to augment the alcoholic strength. English wines need buckets of the stuff.

The yeast for winemaking was traditionally derived from the natural 'bloom' on the grapeskin – a greyish patina of yeast fungus that simply arrives there carried by spores in the air – and was mashed into the grapejuice by barefooted treaders. Nowadays, specially cultured and standardised yeast is added to the winevats to ferment the filtered grapejuice in a more controlled way.

Apart from differences in alcohol content, there are numerous other differences between the multitude of wines. But suffice it for me to say here that red wines get their colour from pigments called anthocyanins in the skins of the black grapes from which they are made. The skins (and pips) also provide tannins which give young wine its mouth-puckering dryness. As the red wine ages, its deep purplish redness becomes lighter and more mahogany-coloured, and its dryness becomes smoother. Other differences of flavour are produced by different varieties of grapes, different soils, and different techniques for maturing the wine. The ability of the young wine to improve with age depends on a subtle combination of different qualities in the grape harvest itself, and in the wine-maker. It's this combination which produces a great vintage – or doesn't, as the case may be.

'It's a naïve domestic burgundy, without any breeding, but I think you'll be amused by its presumption.'

JAMES THURBER

As you'd expect, most white wines are produced from white grapes, the yellowish tinge coming from phenolic compounds in the skins. But surprisingly some white wines are made with black grapes – champagne being the most notable example – in which case the skins have to be separated from the grapejuice before fermentation, to prevent the red pigments from leeching into the wine.

As with red wines, the subtleties of aromatic flavour are determined by the type of grape, climate, technique and skill of the winemaker. The dryness/sweetness of a white wine depends mainly on sugar content,

but also to a limited extent on tannins. As a white wine ages it becomes a darker yellow, and the tannins fade to give a smoother taste.

A good rosé wine is made from black grapes which are left in contact with their skins during fermentation for just long enough for a little red pigment to get into the wine. Cheaper rosés are made by mixing red and white wines together.

And what about sparkling? Where do the bubbles come from? Well, the proper champagne method uses a second fermentation in the bottle to make carbon dioxide, which, because it's corked up firmly, has to dissolve in the wine. It then reappears as bubbles when the cork is popped. But this is a labour-intensive, fiddly procedure (I mean the second fermentation, not the cork-popping – although that can be troublesome enough). So cheaper sparkling wines have the carbon dioxide added artificially, pumped in under pressure, and the bubbles are never quite the same as the real thing.

....

The furthest a champagne cork has ever flown (when released from a bottle 4 feet off the ground) is 177′ 9″, almost 60 yards! The top popper is a certain Professor Emeritus Heinrich Medicus, RPI, who achieved his feat at Woodbury Vineyards Winery, New York on 5 June 1988.

....

SHERRY ....
A white wine fortified with grape spirit (brandy). The deepest and strongest are the olorosos. The driest and lightest are the finos. Amontillados are in between. Much skill goes into the making and blending of sherries.

....

The word 'sherry' comes from Jerez, the region of Spain that produces the world's best sherries. Oddly enough, the British drink ten times as much of the stuff as the Spaniards.

....

PORT ....
The fermentation of red grapejuice is stopped mid-way by adding grape spirit. Thus only part of the sugar is converted to alcohol. The result is a

deep-coloured sweet drink that matures wonderfully on the wood. The vintage is everything with port.

VERMOUTH

Vermouths are fortified wines blended with herbs and other extracts, using age-old, closely guarded, secret recipes. The word 'vermouth' comes from the Bavarian word *vermut* for wormwood, the medicinal herb beloved of absinthe drinkers, but no longer used in modern aperitifs. They are dry or sweet, white or red, depending on the wine base used.

CIDER

Apples provide the sugar for cider, a traditional drink in England and Normandy, and for applejack, which is drunk in New England. (A similar beverage made from pears, called perry, was also popular in these parts, but has now all but vanished into history.) Cider is made in a similar way to wine, but usually with much diluted apple-juice to keep its alcohol content nearer that of beer. However, strong 'vintage' cider can reach the same strength as some wines.

SPIRITS

Distillation is the name of the game. It's the only way to get the alcohol content higher than the 14 per cent at which most yeast cells die (apart from a delinquent British yeast which can stagger on to produce a brew of 22 per cent alcohol!). It involves heating the fermented liquid until most of the alcohol boils off as vapour. By some streak of good fortune (or bad if you're a prohibitionist), this happens before most of the water turns to steam – otherwise distilleries would be better off as power-stations. The alcohol vapour is condensed to a gratifyingly potent 'spirit' which can then be flavoured with different essences, such as juniper berries in gin, or by 'maturing' it in wooden barrels, as with scotch whisky in oak sherry casks. Or left more or less as it is, and called vodka.

WHISKY

Whisky is made by double distillation of fermented grain mash – the grain being primarily malted barley for Scotch; malted and unmalted barley for Irish whiskey (with an 'e'); or corn or rye mash for Canadian or

American whisky (bourbon). The Japanese produce their own quite acceptable versions of Scotch and bourbon. And the Welsh have just re-introduced their own ancient *chwisgi* – a herbal whisky with a hint of the hills.

Malt whisky is matured for 5–20 years in old oaken casks which impart a characteristic local flavour and colour. Blended whisky is made by mixing a blend of malts with newly distilled grain spirit. The mixture is then matured for a minimum of three years in large vats.

The alcoholic strength of most whiskies is 'broken down' with water to about 40 per cent (some cheaper whiskies are bottled at a rather lower alcohol content than this – but still can taste good).

GIN

Gin is also made by double distillation of fermented grain mash, which is then flavoured with essence of juniper and other herb extracts.

London Dry is lightly flavoured compared to the deeper golden coloured Dutch gin.

BRANDY

Distilled from wine, matured in casks, and blended with great subtlety. Good brandy – whether cognac, armagnac, or other types – must come from good wine, and be a long time in cask.

VODKA

Distilled from fermented grain – which can be wheat, corn or rice. (Not potatoes, as is widely believed.) Vodka is a very clean spirit, not blended with anything other than water, and in some types a light herbal or fruit extract. Russian, Polish and Finnish vodkas have a heavier flavour than European vodka from Paris or Warrington.

RUM

Distilled from fermented sugar-cane. Traditionally the dark-coloured demerara rums from Guyana and Jamaica, matured in charred oak barrels, were most popular in Britain. Recently, lighter rums from Puerto Rico and Cuba, matured in plain barrels, and better for mixing in cocktails, have made inroads. Very smart are the rhums agricole, from the French Caribbean.

TEQUILA

Made by double distillation from the fermented juice of a cactus-like plant in Mexico. It was virtually unknown outside the place until the hippies moved in in the mid 1960s.

LIQUEURS

Usually made either by re-distilling.brandy and blending in concoctions of herbs, fruit extracts and sugars or by mixing herbal and fruit essences into neutral grape spirit. There are hundreds of different liqueurs, mostly sweet in taste, and strong in alcohol.

HOW MUCH ALCOHOL IS IN YOUR DRINKS?

BEERS & LAGERS

	% ALC	VOLUME	UNITS
ordinary strength beer/lager	3%	8g/½pt	1
		12g/can	1½
		16g/pt	2
export beer/lager	4%	10g/½pt	1¼
		16g/can	2
		20g/pt	2½
strong beer/lager	5½%	16g/½pt	2
		24g/can	3
		32g/pt	4
extra strength beer/lager	7%	20g/½pt	2½
		32g/can	4
		40g/pt	5

CIDERS

	% ALC	VOLUME	UNITS
average cider	4%	12g/½pt	1½
		24g/pt	3
strong cider	6%	16g/½pt	2
		32g/pt	4

TABLE WINES ....

	% ALC	VOLUME	UNITS
red/white/rose (sweet or dry)	8–10%	av. 8g/glass (pub meas) 56g/bott.	1 7

FORTIFIED WINES ....

sherry/port/vermouth	13–16%	av. 8g/glass (pub meas)	1

LIQUEURS ....

various	15–30%	av. 8g/glass (pub meas)	1

SPIRITS ....

gin/whisky/vodka/brandy/rum (70% proof)	32–40%	8g/single (Eng & Wales) 12g/single (Scot & NI) 240g/bott.	1 1½ 30

(From RCP Report 1987)

WHO DRINKS WHAT AND HOW MUCH?

You'd need to have been living on Mars not to know that the average Brit's love of lager has rocketed over the last decade, and that as a nation we're downing ever bigger lakefuls of wine. But did you know that we're also witnessing a boom in cider drinking? And a miniboom in exotic premixed cocktails? And although draught beer sales are falling away, we're taking home more and more cans of the bitter brew? To say nothing of the high level of interest in the new low-alcohol drinks (more of which in Chapter 14).

Maybe that's a commentary on our society, that people try to get away from everything by getting drunk.

TERRY WOGAN

Altogether, in the course of a year, the average adult in this country gets through about 250 pints of beer or lager (140 litres), about 20 bottles of wine (14 litres), eight litres (1½ gallons) of cider, and about five litres of spirits. Since quite a few people drink much less than that, an awful lot drink an awful lot more!

Our overall consumption can be gleaned from sales figures, but how much are people really drinking? What do we know about who's drinking what? How do men compare with women? Young people with old? The North with the South? And how have things changed over the past decade?

A MAJOR SURVEY

The answers to these questions have just become available (for England and Wales at any rate), thanks to a major government-funded survey of

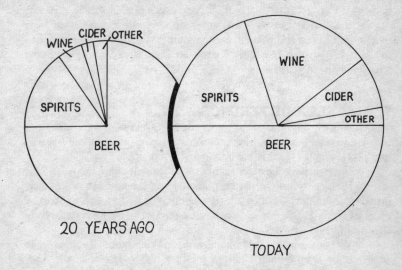

20 YEARS AGO

TODAY

nearly 4000 adults up and down the country, undertaken by the Office of Population Censuses and Surveys.

The OPCS survey was done in 1987, to provide a picture of drinking habits before the change in licensing hours in August 1988. Another survey will be done soon to see whether the new law has had an impact on the amount we drink. The OPCS also conducted a similar survey back in 1978, and this means we can make some interesting comparisons.

In the survey, people were asked about their drinking habits during the previous seven days. No doubt some people couldn't remember too clearly, and others weren't all that keen to tell the whole truth. For some it might have been an unusually heavy week at the bar or the bottle, and for others a strangely abstinent one. But all-in-all, with nearly 4000 people answering the questions, these things tend to even out, and the results amount to the best information we have on who drinks what and how much.

CHANGING TIMES ....

The first thing to say is that, overall, we're drinking no more alcohol now than we did a decade ago. In terms of the number of units the average person drinks in a week, consumption has remained at about nine and a half – that's just less than five pints of beer, or ten glasses of wine.

But that's not to say that consumption has remained static over that period. In fact according to Customs and Excise figures it was rising in the late 1970s, then fell fairly sharply in the early 1980s, and is now steadily on the increase again.

SEX MAKES A DIFFERENCE

That figure of nine and a half units for the average drinker hides the well-known fact that men drink more than women – about three times as much – 14½ units a week compared to just less than five.

But how have the sexes fared over the past decade?

Well, surprisingly perhaps, men have actually cut down their drinking. Admittedly, not by a huge amount – by half a unit a week to be precise (a quarter of a pint of beer or the equivalent), not even statistically significant.

Women, on the other hand, are drinking more. Their average consumption is up by half a unit a week (eg half a glass of wine). And, because they're not such big drinkers as men, that half unit represents a significant increase of over 10 per cent.

LIGHT, MODERATE OR HEAVY

But we're still talking about *the amount the average* man or woman drinks. How about looking at how many of us are light, moderate or heavy drinkers? According to the survey:

'Light' drinking for men is 1–21 units a week. And for women, 1–14 units.

'Moderate' drinking for men is 22–35 units, and 15–25 units for women.

'Fairly heavy' drinking is 36–50 units for men, and 26–35 for women.

'Very heavy' is 51+ and 36+ respectively.

The chart below shows how our drinking habits are broken down by sex (for information on how our sexual habits are broken down by drink *see* pp.80–1 and pp.85–6).

The main medical authorities and health promotion bodies in this country (including the Royal College of Physicians) have agreed on recommended limits for 'sensible' drinking. These are no more than 21 units a week for men, and no more than 14 units a week for women; each with two or three days without any alcohol at all. This corresponds to the

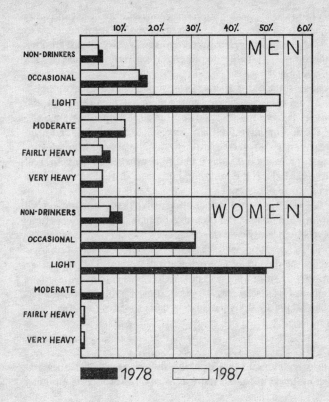

| | 10% | 20% | 30% | 40% | 50% | 60% |

NON-DRINKERS
OCCASIONAL
LIGHT
MODERATE
FAIRLY HEAVY
VERY HEAVY

M E N

NON-DRINKERS
OCCASIONAL
LIGHT
MODERATE
FAIRLY HEAVY
VERY HEAVY

W O M E N

■■■■ 1978   ▭ 1987

'occasional' and 'light' groups in the survey. As you can see from the chart, about one man in four is drinking more than his sensible limit (ie 'moderate', 'fairly heavy' and 'very heavy'); and about one woman in 12 more than hers. These proportions haven't really changed over recent years.

The experts also warn that very heavy drinking – 51 or more units a week for men, or 36 or more for women – is definitely harmful, leading to a whole string of possible health problems (*see* Chapter 8). The chart shows that overall about 6 per cent of all men (nearly one in 16), and 1 per cent (one in a 100) of all women, fall into this category (probably literally!).

YOUNG AND OLD

What these figures don't show is that, for younger people, the proportion of very heavy drinkers is much higher than this – for 18–24-year-old men it's roughly double the overall male rate, and for women of the same age it's multiplied by four times!

Nevertheless, the changes since 1978 are actually quite encouraging from the health point of view. Among young men, between 18 and 24, the percentage of very heavy drinkers is down from 13 to 11 per cent, and the percentage of those drinking more than the sensible limit, has fallen from 48 to 37 per cent – that's down by a fifth. For 18–24-year-old women, very heavy drinking has remained steady (if that's the word!) at 4 per cent, and the percentage exceeding the sensible limit has drifted only slightly upwards, from 15 to 16 per cent.

In the 25–34 age group, about one-third of the men, and one-eighth of the women, drink more than the sensible limits, and these proportions haven't changed significantly over the decade.

Oddly enough, the group who have most markedly increased their proportion exceeding the limit are 35–44-year-old women. The percentage for this age group is up from 8 per cent in 1978 to 12 per cent in 1987 – that's half as much again. Could it be those extra bottles of 'mother's comforter' buried under the family's weekly hatchbackful of groceries I wonder?

HOW OFTEN

The experts also recommend that drinking should be confined to a few separate occasions a week, so that there are two or three days completely

without alcohol. The survey shows that nearly half of all men, and over a quarter of all women, drink on four or more occasions weekly.

The average male drinker has four or five drinking sessions a week, often downing pints in the pub, amounting to an average of just over four units a session – say, two pints. It's all a lot less for women – three or four sessions a week, most often sipping wine at home, averaging two units (that's two glasses of wine) at a sitting.

'I distrust camels – and anyone else who can go for a week without a drink.'

JOE E. LEWIS

And women are slower too. It takes about 20 minutes for our Mr Average to demolish his unit (say, half a pint), but a full half-hour for Ms Average to deal with her unit (perhaps a glass of wine).

WHERE DO PEOPLE DRINK?

Traditionally, men have always favoured drinking in the pub – looking in at lunchtime, and perhaps again after work. The ladies, on the other hand, prefer to take their tipple in the comfort of their own home. But over the past decade there's been a boom in home drinking for men too, so that it now rivals the pub as their favourite watering hole. So, the six-packs of lager are being thrown into the hatchback too!

As far as regional differences are concerned, drinking has always been heaviest in the North of England (and Scotland and Northern Ireland). That is still the case, although such differences are steadily diminishing. Wales is emerging as a high drinking area too. The plaudits for the lowest consumption figures go to East Anglia, the East Midlands and South-west England. The biggest change over the past decade has been in the East Midlands, where there's been a 50 per cent jump in drinking figures, although they remain comparatively low.

CLASSY STUFF

The biggest drinkers have always tended to be those in the 'unskilled manual' group. Hard physical labour can work up a huge thirst, screaming out for long quenching draughts of lager (and having worked on a building site I can speak from experience!). But as unskilled work becomes more and more mechanised and less and less manual, or at least less physical, so

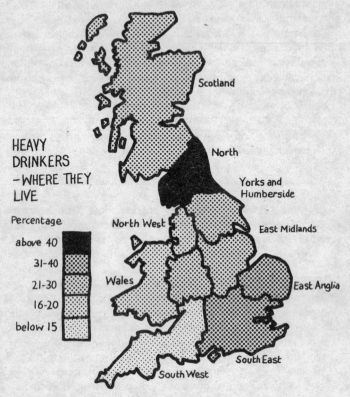

HEAVY
DRINKERS
–WHERE THEY
LIVE

Percentage

above 40
31-40
21-30
16-20
below 15

Scotland

North

Yorks and
Humberside

North West

East Midlands

Wales

East Anglia

South East

South West

Source: Alcohol Concern (1987)

the alcohol consumption by this group is slowly coming down (by about 8 per cent over the past decade). This fall also reflects an overall moderation in men's drinking – the greatest reduction being at the other end of the social scale, among professional men, with a 33 per cent drop. In fact, the only group of men among whom drinking is increasing, and then only slightly, is the semi-skilled non-manual group – clerks, shop-workers, waiters, catering assistants, and so on. No doubt due to all the frustrations of petty bureaucracy!

Among women, the figures from the survey are too small to draw proper conclusions, but there does seem to be more drinking going on in the middle income bracket, and by contrast, as with men, a 33 per cent drop in the professional group.

These changes help to explain the shifts in sales of beer and wine. The beer market, very much male dominated, is stagnant or falling, and the general reduction of men's drinking in most social groups, particularly the traditionally beer-swilling manual workers, has had its effect. The wine market is on the up and up, however. The survey shows that the average number of units of wine has nearly doubled over the decade, for both sexes equally. It seems likely that the extra drinking by women in the middle income bracket is mainly a combination of the new pub-going independent single woman and the married mum with a few bottles of Spanish white in her supermarket trolley.

DOWN THE HATCH!
immediate effects on the body

'I always wake up at the crack of ice.'

JOE E. LEWIS

Unlike food, alcohol does *not* have to be digested before it can be absorbed into the bloodstream. Most nutrients – such as proteins, fats and complex carbohydrates – consist of large molecules that have to be broken down chemically into much smaller molecules before they can pass through the cell layer lining the gut and thence into the blood capillaries that enmesh the stomach and intestines. This process of digestion needs enzymes in the form of digestive juices, and it takes hours to be completed.

Not so alcohol.

Alcohol molecules are already small, and pass easily and quickly into the bloodstream. In fact, believe it or not, some alcohol gets into your blood before you've even put your lips to the glass! A minute quantity of alcohol vapour is inhaled – rather more if you're drinking spirits, especially neat brandy or malt – and is absorbed into the bloodstream through the nasal membranes and lungs. The classic brandy glass is specially designed so that the vapour from the warm brandy can be sniffed in to give you a satisfyingly rapid 'hit'.

Once the stuff is in your mouth, a little more alcohol is absorbed into the bloodstream, through the lining of your tongue and cheeks – but again only a tiny amount at this stage, because the drink doesn't usually linger long enough.

Then down your gullet it goes and into your stomach – where quite a lot of the alcohol is absorbed through the stomach wall. You might begin to notice this about 10–20 minutes after a drink. The stronger the drink, the faster this initial gastric absorption – up to a point. If you swallow a very strong slug, such as neat spirit, it acts as a gastric irritant, and your stomach reacts by secreting gastric juice in an effort to dilute and soothe

the irritation. This slows down the absorption of the alcohol. So, medium-strength drinks work fastest – sherry, vermouth, port, madeira and spirit/mixer combinations such as gin-and-tonic or whisky-and-soda.

'Have a madeira m'dear, it's really much nicer than beer.'

MICHAEL FLANDERS

But most of the alcohol is absorbed in the next part of its journey – in the duodenum and small intestine. This is the part that specialises in absorption – 20ft of tubing with a huge inner surface area through which most digested nutrients and other substances, including alcohol, pass into the bloodstream.

The speed at which this happens depends on how soon the stomach squeezes its contents out through the pyloric valve and into the duodenum. This begins within minutes if you drink on an empty stomach, but again, strong spirits slow down the process by delaying this gastric emptying. Food is the main cause of delayed emptying and slow absorption of alcohol. Eating something, especially something containing fat or protein, means that the stomach has to churn it about a bit with gastric juice to break it up and start the process of digestion. This takes time, and it may be an hour or so before the valve opens and the food and alcohol mixture can enter the small intestine. Hence the oft-quoted advice to 'line your stomach' with a snack, such as a cheese roll or a ham sandwich, or even a glass of milk and a biscuit or two, to prevent yourself from getting too tiddly too quickly. Virtually all the alcohol will still eventually get into your bloodstream, but not in such a rush. And this delay means that the peak level of alcohol in your blood will only reach about a quarter of the level it would on an empty stomach.

BLOOD IN YOUR ALCOHOL STREAM.......................
Because alcohol dissolves easily in water (all alcoholic drinks are solutions of alcohol in water, or vice versa), it is carried in your blood circulation, dissolved in the plasma, the aqueous solution that the blood cells float in.

The amount of alcohol in the blood is usually measured in terms of its level or concentration. This is the Blood Alcohol Concentration or BAC.

BAC TO BASICS

The circulation rapidly distributes the alcohol all round the body – to the brain, lungs, heart, liver, kidneys, and other organs. The higher the water content of each particular type of tissue, the more alcohol it can take up. The brain, for instance, having a soft blancmange-like consistency, contains a lot of water, and rapidly attracts a large amount of the available alcohol.

By contrast, adipose tissue (bodyfat), being highly fatty, has a very low water content, and virtually refuses to accept any alcohol.

Between these two extremes are tissues like muscle, liver, heart and other organs, which have a medium water content and take up the alcohol fairly well. For example, your muscles are really surprisingly watery and the alcohol enters them readily.

The alcohol balance between the blood and these aqueous tissues equalises within a few minutes, so that the level in your brain, for instance, soon matches that in your blood.

SMALL IS BOOZEFUL

Since muscles make up such a large proportion of your body weight, they are particularly important in determining the amount of 'room' the alcohol has to be distributed in, and hence the concentration of alcohol in your blood – your BAC.

For example, if you're a big muscular person, any given quantity of alcohol will have a large amount of muscle to occupy, and hence the level in your tissues, and your BAC, will be relatively lower than if you were a small, skinny person. Hence most men, being generally larger and more muscular than women tend to be able to 'hold their drink' rather better. Smaller people (by which I mean lighter people) get drunker quicker, because their alcohol level, or BAC, builds up that much faster.

But weight alone isn't the only consideration.

Question: If a man and woman of *the same weight* drink the same quantity of alcohol on an empty stomach, who will have the higher BAC?
Answer: The woman. But why?

The reason is that, weight for weight, women tend to be fatter than men. That is, they have relatively more bodyfat – about 25 per cent of the average woman being fat, compared with about 15 per cent of the average man. And since bodyfat doesn't accept much alcohol, it all gets concentrated in the other tissues, including the bloodstream. Hence women, with relatively less of the other tissues, will have a higher BAC, and they, too, tend to get drunker quicker.

Which can be a good thing or a bad thing, depending on your circumstances.

'One more drink and I'll be under the host.'
DOROTHY PARKER

HOW HIGH, HOW FAST? . . . .

Obviously, the more alcohol you drink, the higher will go your BAC. But speed is a factor too. Alcohol is slowly and steadily eliminated from the body, and therefore you have to take in alcohol faster than that in order to raise your BAC. In practice this is not difficult – if you drink at the rate of, say, more than half a pint of ordinary bitter or lager (or a glass of wine) an hour, your alcohol level will continue to rise. If you drink more slowly than that, it will fall. Worth remembering if you're driving.

Let's just look at your alcohol level, your BAC, after you've had a few quick drinks – say three halves of lager – on a virtually empty stomach (apart from your usual bagful of smokey-bacon-flavoured crisps). All the alcohol in the lager (about 8 grams in each half) will enter your bloodstream fairly rapidly, and will reach a peak BAC in about 30–60 minutes, assuming you were pretty parched and quaffed the lot in quick succession.

As I've said, the precise level of this BAC will depend on your weight and sex. So, if you're an average man weighing about 11 stones (70kg), the 24 grams of alcohol you've just swallowed will be distributed throughout your non-fat tissue (about 85 per cent of you, or about 60kg). Well I can spare you the mental arithmetic by telling you that, since a kilogram of non-fat tissue (such as blood) occupies about 800ml volume, that works out at a BAC of about 60mg/100ml.

In other words, those three halves of lager give you a BAC of about 60mg% after about one hour. Notice there are lots of 'abouts' about, because it's all very approximate. There are so many imponderables that it's impossible to predict precisely what your BAC will be, without a vanload of laboratory equipment. But of course, as the police know well enough, it's easy enough to evaluate the BAC once the alcohol's in your system!

If you happen to be heavier than 70kg, your BAC one hour after the three lagers will be a bit lower than 60mg%. And if you're lighter than

How your weight and sex affect your BAC

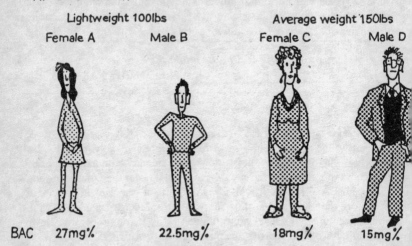

AFTER ONE UNIT

Lightweight 100lbs   Average weight 150lbs

Female A   Male B   Female C   Male D

BAC   27mg%   22.5mg%   18mg%   15mg%

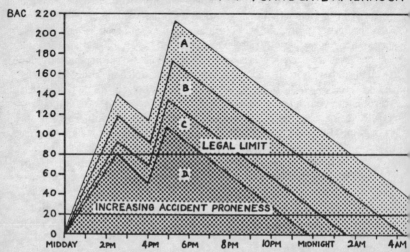

AFTER 5 UNITS AT LUNCHTIME AND 4 UNITS LATE AFTERNOON

70kg, especially if you're a woman (with relatively less muscle), your BAC could be quite a bit higher.

   To make all this rather easier to grasp, the experts have come up with the simple concept of a standard 'unit' of alcohol. It means we don't have to think in terms of how many grams, or fluid ounces, or rods, poles or perches of alcohol in any particular drink in order to try to predict the BAC, and hence its effect on us.

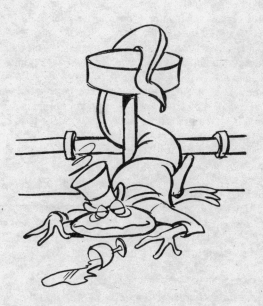

TO THE BRAIN...

'I'm not as think as you drunk I am.'

Anon

Why is alcohol so enjoyable?

Contrary to popular belief, alcohol is *not* a stimulant. Indeed, true stimulants, like coffee and tea, are used to counteract its effects. Alcohol is in fact a depressant – it slows down the electrical impulses that control our moods, thoughts and actions – usually in that order. And, in high doses, it can suppress or even inactivate some of our most vital physiological functions – like consciousness, swallowing, coughing and even breathing. To put it bluntly, alcohol is a general anaesthetic. Enough of it can lay you out cold – very cold.

And not surprisingly, it's also an analgesic (painkiller), interfering with the nerve centres for pain and touch in the mid-brain. Indeed, until the use of ether in the nineteenth century, it was more or less the only widely available analgesic/anaesthetic outside China (they had opium). Many is the lacerated limb that's been amputated using nothing more than a tourniquet, a saw, a few glugs of gin and a prayer.

So, how is it that this 'depressant' can be so exhilarating? The reason is that one of the first effects it has on your brain is to reduce the activity of your frontal lobes. Those are what you should have behind your forehead and between your temples, and they are mainly concerned with what the psychologists delight in describing as higher cognitive processes and social control. When alcohol hits your frontal lobes, they do a sort of striptease – and the first things to go are your inhibitions.

You talk a little more easily, and a little louder. You laugh more readily, you touch more casually, you are more excitable. At the same time, you're less anxious, less tense, less preoccupied and less discriminating. You feel good. Relaxed, convivial and engaging. It's the perfect social lubricant – it sets everyone up for living and loving.

'Drink makes me feel rosy all over – and it makes her feel me all over.'

MORGAN DANVERS

At least, that's if you're basically in a good mood, and in good company. But if you happen to be seething with pent-up anger, resentment, frustration, aggression, hatred and other unpleasantries, then drink will release those ugly emotions, with predictable and unpredictable consequences for any nearby life, limb and property. Alcohol, I'm afraid, is all too often a drug of violence.

Bad company magnifies the mayhem. From football hooligans to lager louts, the urge to vandalise and terrorise is powered by youth and the anonymity of the herd, and fuelled with alcohol. The injury and damage caused by alcohol-related violence is incalculable (*see* p.102).

But back to your frontal lobes. And another drink or two . . .

The next nerve connections to be affected are those linking one thought with another – associations. Almost without realising it you find it harder to think of more than one thing at a time, and to remember what's been said or done. You may start to lose the thread of the conversation, or you may be so engrossed that you lose track of what's going on around you. Suddenly half-an-hour or an hour has vanished, most pleasurably, but you can't actually recall a thing about it. Or at least, not very much. Nor indeed can you be bothered to – because your powers of concentration are getting more diluted by the minute.

Your mind is beginning to float free. You say what you're thinking, rather more than you think what you're saying. And you say what you're *feeling* too. And what you're feeling is g-o-o-d.

What is not so good is that your ability to judge movement, speed and distance, is beginning to be impaired – without you realising it. As you relax more and more, and let yourself go, your cortex, or grey matter, where movement, speed and distance are judged, begins to take it easy and get a bit lackadaisical. Just as you're feeling nice feelings – you're becoming more accident-prone. Another drink or two and people start bumping into you. Whoops! You spilt a drop then, never mind, it's got to go to the cleaners anyway.

You begin, too, to have a little trouble getting your teeth and tongue round the odd word or two. Just the particully . . . pritically . . . part-ic-u-lar-ly diffcut ones.

'*O God that men should put an enemy in their mouths to steal away their brains.*'

WILLIAM SHAKESPEARE

The lack of co-ordination is due to the depressant effect of alcohol on the cerebellar pathways. The cerebellum is the 'little brain' below your cerebral hemispheres, just behind the point where the spinal cord enters the mid brain. Its function is to control the co-ordination of muscles all over the body and make the necessary fine adjustments to keep you upright. In other words it co-ordinates balance, posture and movement.

It does this by constantly monitoring the position of all your main moving parts. Your muscles and joints have in-built strain-gauges – sensors – which constantly send messages to the cerebellum informing it of the degree of tension or stretch occurring at any given moment. The cerebellum acts like an on-board computer, constantly calculating the angles of joints and the directions of movements, linking these calculations in with sights and sounds, and with data from the balance organs in the inner ears, so that subconsciously you 'know' how your body is deployed in space.

This means, for instance, that when you want to scratch your nose, you don't have to decide precisely how much you've got to contract your biceps, or relax your triceps, or lift your deltoid, or alternately flex and extend your index finger. You simply think, 'My nose is itching. I will scratch it,' and it happens.

So, what does alcohol do to this splendid arrangement? Well, just as in the higher brain, it depresses nerve transmission, and reduces the information flowing backwards and forwards within the cerebellum, and between that part of the brain and the others. The result is the unco-ordination most of us are all too familiar with. Your nose itches, so you scratch your eyeball. You stagger backwards, knock someone's drink off the bar, and apodglise perfooshly.

Then you buy another round or two . . .

By this stage, you know you've had a few too many. You might regard yourself as pleasantly tight, a little merry, a bit sloshed, perhaps

even rather drunk. But you're OK. You can handle it. At least, that's how it seems to you – so you have another drink.

In fact by now, you're beginning to see double. Things are swimming a bit. You go to the loo, and it seems like a major expedition into alien territory. On the way back to civilisation, you find yourself sliding down the wall. You decide it's time to leave. You can't be bothered to say goodbye, but you manage to remember your coat, and then, suddenly, you're out on the street, lurching from one side of the pavement to the other, and you don't feel so good.

Being a tidy person, you're sick in the gutter. And, feeling a little better, you make your way home . . . somehow.

'A man is never drunk if he can lay on the floor without holding on.'

JOE E. LEWIS

This little scenario may not ring quite true for you, but it will for an awful lot of people. I can describe it reasonably accurately because I've found myself in that situation on more than one occasion (and not just as a medical student either!).

Someone who's got to that stage is, needless to say, completely and utterly plastered. Their blood alcohol concentration (BAC) as they leave the pub or party is probably around 200mg%. The legal limit for driving is 80mg%, so they've got about two and a half times that amount in their bloodstream. And yet a great many people in that situation get into their car and drive home – even though they know they've had a skinful. What they don't seem to realise is just how drunk they are. But that's not surprising, because when you drink you lose your judgement, more with every drink, including the ability to know just how much you've drunk and how much judgement you've lost.

Below is a table of the effects of different amounts of drink. The chart relates to a man of average build. For the average woman, the effects will occur at lower levels of alcohol.

BAC......EFFECT

BAC	EFFECT
20mg%	More relaxed. Pleasant calmness. A feeling of wellbeing.
30mg%	More talkative. Losing some inhibitions. Driving skills beginning to be impaired. Risk of accidents starts to increase.

50mg%	Carefree. Inhibitions going fast. Judgement beginning to be affected. Decision-making skills start to deteriorate.
80mg%	Hand-eye co-ordination now markedly diminished. Accident rate doubled. Legal limit for driving.
100mg%	Obvious deterioration in physical and social control. Clumsy and emotional.
160mg%	Swaying and slurring. Obviously drunk. Twice the legal limit for driving.
200mg%	Some staggering, double vision and perhaps vomiting.
300mg%	Grossly intoxicated and semicomatose.
400mg%	Unconscious and unrousable. Breathing shallow. Cough reflex lost. High risk of suffocating on inhaled vomit.
500mg%	Death likely from paralysis of breathing.

BALANCING YOUR BAC

So how can you keep your BAC at just the level you want it? Not too low for you to relax and enjoy yourself. And not so high that you can't drive home. Or, if you've got a lift, that you have to be carried to it.

The answer is to pace yourself, to drink at the right rate for the job. Which means knowing how many units to drink in, say, an hour at the local, or at a four-hour party.

As I've said, it'll depend on your sex and weight. So here are some tables, based on figures published by the Scottish Health Education Group, to save you the trouble of fumbling with a calculator in the middle of an important tête-à-tête. All you have to do is choose the level to aim at depending on how you want to feel, and drink at the pace suggested. The quantities refer to units of alcohol.

NICE 'N' EASY (BAC 50)
You are feeling pleasant, relaxed and carefree.

MEN	In 1 hr	In 2 hrs	In 3 hrs	In 4 hrs	In 5 hrs
under 11st	2	3	4	4½	5
11–13st	2½	4	5	5½	6
over 13st	3	4½	5½	5½	6

WOMEN	In 1 hr	In 2 hrs	In 3 hrs	In 4 hrs	In 5 hrs
under 9st	1½	2	2½	3	3½
9–11st	2	2½	3½	4	4½
over 11st	2½	3	4	5	5½

AT THE LIMIT (BAC 80)

You feel confident and uninhibited. But your risk of an accident is double. This is the legal limit for driving.

MEN	In 1 hr	In 2 hrs	In 3 hrs	In 4 hrs	In 5 hrs
under 11st	3½	4	5	5½	6½
11–13st	4	5	6	6½	7½
over 13st	5	6	7	7½	8

WOMEN	In 1 hr	In 2 hrs	In 3 hrs	In 4 hrs	In 5 hrs
under 9st	2½	3	3½	3½	4
9–11st	3	3½	4½	4½	5½
over 11st	3½	4½	5½	5½	6

MAKING MERRY (BAC 120)

You're actually feeling rather tiddly – excitable, emotional and not-a-little impulsive. I reckon this is just about the best BAC for celebrating and really enjoying yourself, as long as you've got a lift home.

MEN	In 1 hr	In 2 hrs	In 3 hrs	In 4 hrs	In 5 hrs
under 11st	5½	6	6½	7	7½
11–13st	6	7	8	8½	9
over 13st	7½	8½	9	9½	10

WOMEN	In 1 hr	In 2 hrs	In 3 hrs	In 4 hrs	In 5 hrs
under 9st	3½	4	4½	4½	5
9–11st	4½	5	5½	5½	6
over 11st	5	6	6½	6½	7

WHERE NEXT?

So, once it's got into your blood, brain and brawn – where does the alcohol go from there?

Well, some gets lost in your breath, since it diffuses out from the blood capillaries in your lungs for some time after your last drink. This could be less than an hour if you've only had a little, or several hours if you're fairly tanked up. The alcohol on your breath has a faintly fruity aroma, and the more you've drunk the stronger it is. But any stories you've heard about a really heavy boozer's breath catching fire are apocryphal, the alcohol vapour is very damp and never strong enough to reach flashpoint.

The concentration of alcohol in your breath parallels the level in your bloodstream, and this simple fact is made much use of by the police with their notorious breathalyser (see p.109).

A small amount is eliminated by your kidneys. As with the breath, the concentration in your urine parallels the BAC, and again police may use a urine test to assess your alcohol status.

An even smaller amount is lost in your sweat and faeces. As far as I know, the police haven't got around to using either of these as drink-driving specimens yet – but it can't be long. Incidentally, a favourite Finnish way of sobering up is by sweating it out in the sauna.

But by far the most important way alcohol is removed from the body – the way about 90 per cent of it is dealt with – is by breaking it down chemically in the liver. This large soft dark-red organ is in the top right-hand side of the abdomen, protected by the rib-cage. It's the body's main chemical processing plant, and it contains scores of different enzymes, each capable of triggering particular chemical reactions converting substances from one to another.

The liver is the first port of call for blood leaving the capillary network surrounding the stomach and intestines. This is essential because many of the substances absorbed from food and drink would be toxic to the brain and other organs if they weren't quickly broken down in the liver – a process called detoxification. Alcohol is one of those potentially toxic substances, and it's broken down by an enzyme called alcohol dehydrogenase, eventually to carbon dioxide and water.

The first step is oxidation to acetaldehyde. Ironically, this is very much more toxic than alcohol, but fortunately it isn't usually around long enough to cause problems – usually nausea, vomiting, flushing and a feeling of utter dread. Instead, it's rapidly oxidised a stage further to acetic acid - none other than good old harmless vinegar – and that in turn is quickly turned into carbon dioxide and water.

Interestingly, there are a few people who don't have enough of the enzyme triggering the second stage, and acetaldehyde starts to build up whenever they drink alcohol. The symptoms are so unpleasant that these people usually go out of their way to avoid alcohol. The Japanese are rather short of this enzyme and, as a race, are not very keen on drinking – suffering bouts of nausea and flushing if they do.

The same chemistry is used to help some people with alcohol dependence. They are asked to take a drug called disulfiram (Antabuse), which has the effect of blocking the action of that second enzyme. If they then succumb to a drink, the resulting build-up of acetaldehyde makes its presence felt extremely unpleasantly. So the disulfiram acts as a remarkably effective deterrent.

TIME TO SOBER UP

As soon as alcohol enters your bloodstream, your liver gets to work. But the chemical process is not instantaneous. It takes time – and the speed at which it happens varies considerably from person to person.

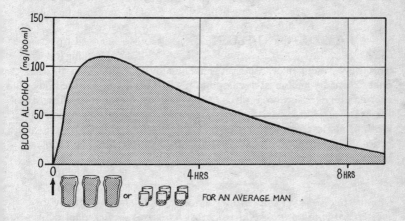

For regular drinkers, for instance, it tends to be faster than for those who only have the occasional little snifter. This is because the drinker's liver enzymes are rather better trained at coping with the stuff. But this is only true up to a point. Once the drinker's liver starts to become damaged (a slow and insidious process), then its efficiency falls off, and it takes longer and longer to clear the alcohol from the bloodstream. So, although a typical heavy drinker may appear to 'hold his drink' quite well, in fact his liver may be struggling hard to get rid of it – and perhaps taking up to four times as long as the average person to do so.

Another factor governing the speed at which we eliminate alcohol is genetics. We inherit the tendency to be fast, slow or middling. Identical twins do it at more or less the same speed – unless one happens to be a chronic boozer and the other teetotal.

But apart from the effects of 'training' and genetics, the speed with which we clear alcohol from our bloodstream is roughly constant. On average, we can remove about 15mg of alcohol per 100ml of blood per hour. That's roughly equivalent to one unit of alcohol (ie one standard drink, such as a glass of wine or half a pint of beer) each hour.

If an averagely-built (70kg or 11st) man has three quick pints (six units of alcohol) on an empty stomach, his blood alcohol concentration (BAC) will peak at over 100mg per 100ml 30–60 minutes after imbibing. That's well over the legal limit for driving – which is 80mg per 100ml. Then his BAC will start to drop at the rate of about 15mg per 100ml every hour. So it'll take another one and a half hours before he is legally 'safe' to drive – altogether over two hours after his last gulp.

A GLASSFUL OF CALORIES

This whole metabolic sequence, catalysed by liver enzymes, releases energy (usually measured as calories). It's as though you were burning a fuel – and indeed alcohol is often used as just that, in the form of meths, for example. Alcohol has quite a high calorie content – each gram of alcohol, just over a millilitre, or half a thimbleful, produces seven calories. Weight for weight, that's half as much again as carbohydrates, and only a little less than fat.

> *Alcohol's very fattening . . . I was, like, a teenager*
> *growing up, constantly battling with my weight and I*
> *never thought that it might be that – you know, it*
> *could be the drink that was doing it. I always assumed*
> *it was the food.*
>
> KIM WILDE

So a pint of ordinary beer or lager, with about 16g of alcohol in it, provides 112 calories just from the alcohol, and with its other ingredients, a total of 180 calories. Strong beer has double the alcohol and nearly double the calorie content. It's easy to see how four or five pints a day can soon result in a beer gut.

Even a glass of dry white wine (4fl.oz or 113ml) contains about 75 calories – so two glasses a day could account for about 10 per cent of an average woman's daily calorie intake.

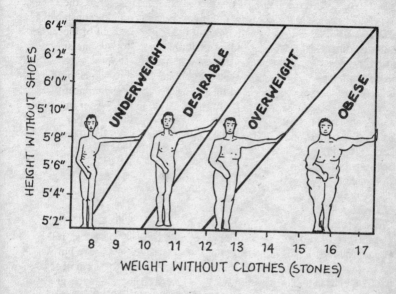

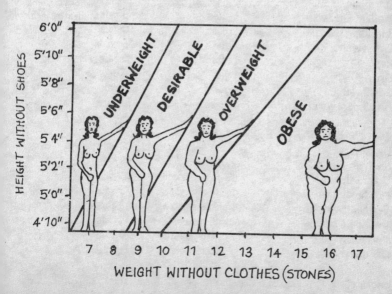

HOW MANY CALORIES IN YOUR FAVOURITE TIPPLE?

BEER & LAGER

Bitter (ordinary)	1 pint (568ml)	180 cals
Keg bitter	1 pint	175 cals
Export bitter	1 pint	250 cals
Strong ale	1 pint	400 cals
Low-alcohol bitter	1 pint	120 cals
No-alcohol bitter	1 pint	100 cals
Lager (ordinary)	1 pint	160 cals
Lager (strong)	1 pint	400 cals
Low-alcohol lager	1 pint	100 cals
No-alcohol lager	1 pint	80 cals

CIDER

Cider (ordinary)	1 pint	200 cals
Cider (special vat)	1 pint	250 cals
Cider (vintage)	1 pint	350 cals

TABLE WINES

Dry white	1 glass (4fl.oz)	75 cals
Medium dry white	1 glass	90 cals
Sparkling white	1 glass	90 cals
Sweet white	1 glass	100 cals
Rosé	1 glass	80 cals
Dry red	1 glass	80 cals
Sweet red	1 glass	95 cals
No-alcohol wines	1 glass	30 cals

FORTIFIED WINES & APERITIFS

Dry sherry	1 small schooner	55 cals
Medium sherry	1 small schooner	60 cals
Cream sherry	1 small schooner	65 cals
Port (average)	1 pub measure	75 cals
Vermouth extra dry	1 pub measure	55 cals
Vermouth bianco	1 pub measure	75 cals
Vermouth rosso	1 pub measure	80 cals
Campari	1 pub measure	115 cals

SPIRITS

Gin	1 single	50 cals
Whisky	1 single	50 cals
Brandy	1 single	50 cals
Vodka	1 single	50 cals
Rum	1 single	50 cals
Tequila	1 single	50 cals
Southern Comfort	1 single	80 cals

LIQUEURS

Liqueurs (average)	1 pub measure	80 cals

CHAPTER EIGHT
LASTING DAMAGE

'Death is nature's way of telling you to slow down.'
Graffito, London

Quite apart from the immediate effects of drink – some desirable, others less so – we can't escape the sad fact that, if we imbibe too much alcohol, too often, and for too long, it will cause damage to several quite important parts of our body – like our brain, nervous system, liver, heart, circulation, and sex organs – not necessarily in that order.

And the even sadder fact is that this damage is all too often permanent.

After all, if you think about it, the human body was not designed to withstand the sorts of doses of alcohol so many people subject it to. Although alcohol does occur in nature, in over-ripe fruit for instance, and the human liver is capable of making an enzyme specifically to deal with it, we humans simply haven't had time to evolve an effective defence against its use in relatively high doses over, say, a decade or two. The few thousand years that we've been drinking booze of various sorts is the blink of an eye in evolutionary terms. As a result, many of our vital organs and tissues are especially vulnerable to alcohol, and sooner or later succumb. Usually sooner rather than later.

In the early stages of damage, full recovery may still be possible if the alcohol is stopped. This is especially the case with younger people, say under 40. But more often than not the cells struggle on and are eventually killed by the alcohol, leaving scarred tissue. Needless to say, tissue and organs that are scarred don't do their job so well, and their owner is likely to run into serious trouble.

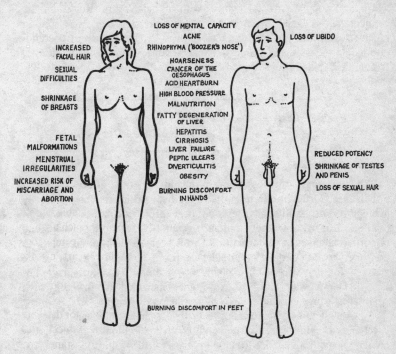

LOSS OF MENTAL CAPACITY
ACNE
RHINOPHYMA ('BOOZER'S NOSE')

INCREASED
FACIAL HAIR

SEXUAL
DIFFICULTIES

SHRINKAGE
OF BREASTS

FETAL
MALFORMATIONS

MENSTRUAL
IRREGULARITIES

INCREASED RISK OF
MISCARRIAGE AND
ABORTION

HOARSENESS
CANCER OF THE
OESOPHAGUS
ACID HEARTBURN
HIGH BLOOD PRESSURE
MALNUTRITION
FATTY DEGENERATION
OF LIVER
HEPATITIS
CIRRHOSIS
LIVER FAILURE
PEPTIC ULCERS
DIVERTICULITIS
OBESITY

BURNING DISCOMFORT
IN HANDS

LOSS OF LIBIDO

REDUCED POTENCY

SHRINKAGE OF TESTES
AND PENIS

LOSS OF SEXUAL HAIR

BURNING DISCOMFORT IN FEET

LOSING YOUR MIND

'Doctor, I seem to be losing my memory.'
'Oh really? When did you first notice this?'
'Notice what, doctor?'

The brain is highly susceptible to the effects of alcohol – and this simple fact accounts very largely for its universal popularity.

But it's also vulnerable to alcohol's long-term effects. And although obvious damage may take years to become apparent, the process can begin within a matter of months.

Research has shown that long-term drinking shrivels up the neuronal connections linking nerve cells with each other. These extremely tiny sub-microscopic filaments normally pass messages backwards and forwards and keep each cell in touch with its neighbours. But when the connections are lost, the brain loses its ability to encode information efficiently, so that not only is recall more difficult, but also it becomes impossible to 'associate' properly – that is, consciously or unconsciously, to link ideas, perceptions, thoughts, memories, and actions.

'I drink. Therefore I . . . ummm.'

MORGAN DANVERS

Amazingly, this loss of brain function has little effect on overall intelligence. Ordinary IQ tests on young heavy drinkers show typically average results – and similar tests on most chronic alcoholics show minimal loss. But we now know that such general IQ tests often mask some important changes in performance. This is because most of the questions are 'word-based', and verbal intelligence is one of the last faculties to be affected by alcohol (which explains why writers like Scott Fitzgerald, Ernest Hemingway and Dylan Thomas managed to produce such stimulating works even after years of very heavy drinking).

But if the tests are tailored to detect changes in such things as psychomotor skills (speed of reaction, co-ordination and hand-eye judgment), visual intelligence (including pattern recognition), non-verbal abstract thought (reasoning with shapes, predicting position from speed and direction) and short-term memory, then a very different story emerges.

People who regularly drink in the danger zone – that's more than 50 units a week for men, or more than 35 for women – show marked deterioration in these crucial skills, and as you'd expect, the higher their dose of alcohol, the more severe this loss of brain function. Now remember, I'm not talking about testing people under the influence. These results are for people who have a blood alcohol concentration of zero. They are stark cold sober.

Perhaps it's not surprising from what I've said about the neurotoxic effect of alcohol that heavy drinking causes this kind of impairment. But research is now showing that even so-called moderate drinking can lead to detectable deficits in these all-important abilities and judgements. It's now becoming apparent that regular drinkers in the warning zone (36–50 units a week for men; 22–35 for women) are likely to perform less

well at psychomotor skills and visual intelligence tests. And remember –
this is when they don't have a drop of alcohol in their system.

You can imagine what this means in the real world. It means that
anyone who drinks at that level and is involved in any driving, designing,
engineering or sport – in fact any of a whole range of skills and activities –
is likely to be performing less accurately, less thoroughly, less
methodically, less skilfully and less intelligently. To put it bluntly, they are
more slapdash.

But the really worrying thing is that they are also unlikely to
appreciate this themselves, because they are also less analytical. The
difference that being a drinker makes may not be all that gross. Indeed it
may be quite subtle. But difference there is, and it's likely to be other
people who notice it first – usually through a fall-off in the quality of the
drinker's work. It becomes increasingly apparent to others that the regular drinker is slowly and insidiously losing his or her touch.

That's the bad news. The good news is that the loss of these skills
and abilities can be reversed if you lay off the booze, or at least cut down.
Younger people especially stand a very good chance of recovering their
full potential if they reduce their level of drinking to the safe range.
People over about 40 are much less able to regain their previous mental
agility – but they can certainly improve their skills by moderating their
alcohol intake. And tests show that this recovery can be detected within a
few weeks of cutting down.

But the longer very heavy drinking continues, the less likely are
the chances of a return to full function – for the simple reason that the
alcohol will have caused irreversible damage to the brain.

BRAIN DAMAGE

It has been known since the last century that the brains of chronic
alcoholics weigh less than normal and show visible signs of shrinkage.
More recently, special X-rays have revealed that the space between the
brain substance and the inner surface of the skull is increased in long-term
heavy drinkers. The grooves between the convolutions of the cerebral
cortex are wider than they should be, and the cavities within the brain are
larger. In other words, brain tissue has been lost.

Post mortem examinations of the brains of drinkers who have been
killed in accidents show some thinning of their normal grey matter –
especially of their frontal lobes (the parts of the cortex that do all the
higher cognitive association and are responsible for judgement and control). Grey matter consists of neurones (nerve cell bodies), and once

neurones are lost, they're gone for ever. The brain can't replace them. Hence the gaps in the wrinkles of the brain surface.

What's more, when neurones go, their long filaments – which form the internal network of nerve connections deep inside the brain – go with them. It's their loss that explains those widening cavities.

In the last few years body-scanners have become available, and these amazing new diagnostic wonders have allowed us to see into the brains of drinkers who are still alive – the likes of you and me. A scanner works by rotating slowly around a person's head, and taking a series of low-dose narrow-beam X-ray readings which are fed into a computer. The computer amalgamates the hundreds of different readings into a composite picture which represents a cross-section of the person's head. Very recently, researchers have undertaken surveys of the general population using a brain-scanner, and they have revealed a worryingly large number of people with varying degrees of the sort of brain-tissue loss that I've been describing.

At the same time as they did the scan, the researchers also asked their subjects about their drinking habits. And, once again, the results point to a clear link between the level of alcohol consumption, the number of years of drinking at that level, the age of the drinker, and the amount of brain damage. The heavier the drinking, the longer it's been going on, and the older the drinker, the more brain damage is seen on the scanner screen.

But the really disturbing thing revealed by these scanner surveys is that even relatively moderate drinkers (in the warning zone) often have detectable changes in their brains when compared to lifelong 'sensible' drinkers.

LIVER LITTLE LONGER

It's that quiet, unassuming, but absolutely vital workhorse, the liver, that always bears the brunt of alcohol's toxic effects. Not only does it have to do virtually all the work of removing this alien chemical from the bloodstream, but it's also the only organ that is thoroughly soaked in the highest concentrations of alcohol that each and every drinking occasion produces. In other words, it's right in the front-line – the first and most important defence against the onslaught – and, not surprisingly, casualties are high.

Most people have heard of cirrhosis of the liver – and they know that it's a serious disease that can often lead to death from jaundice and liver failure. But it's a mistake to think that cirrhosis and other forms of alcohol-induced injury to the liver only happen to chronic alcoholics. The

> *'It costs money to die of cirrhosis of the liver.'*
> P. G. WODEHOUSE

evidence points clearly to the disturbing fact that even heavy social drinkers can have quite severe liver damage.

Under the microscope, the liver consists of strings of liver cells, tightly packed together, and bathed in the blood which has come straight from the stomach and intestines, via the portal vein. It is this high blood content which gives the organ its dark red colour. The liver has many jobs, but essentially it's a chemical processing plant, and one of its main tasks is to treat the blood arriving from the guts, to ensure that as many toxic substances as possible are removed or rendered harmless before they are allowed to pass round the general circulation to all other parts of the body. Food and drink contains so many potential poisons that, without a liver to 'de-toxify' the substances extracted by digestion and absorption from the gut, we would be lucky to survive a single plate of roast beef and Yorkshire pudding!

To do this job, the liver cells have the remarkable ability to produce a whole range of different enzymes on demand. When faced with a particular substance to be dealt with, the liver cells respond by selecting the appropriate enzyme blueprint in their production unit, and then switch on, pouring the enzyme into the brew within their own cell bodies.

In the case of alcohol, when the liver cells find themselves soaked with the stuff, they automatically switch on the production of the enzyme alcohol dehydrogenase. This mixes with the alcohol inside the cells and converts it first to acetaldehyde (even more toxic than alcohol!), then to acetic acid (vinegar), and finally to carbon dioxide, water and energy (calories).

All this is a continuous process, and goes on for as long as there is alcohol in the bloodstream, removing it at a rate equivalent to one unit of alcohol each hour (*see* p.61).

So far, so good. So what's the problem?

The problem is that, although we have the capability of detoxifying alcohol (probably because man, being an omnivore, eating ripe fruit, has lived with tiny quantities of natural alcohol for as long as he's been in existence), our liver cells were never designed to cope with the unnaturally high doses, for so many years, that many of us subject them to. The toxic effect of alcohol damages the very cells that are working so hard to protect the rest of the body. They are true martyrs and unfortunately die in large numbers. When they do so they are replaced at first by fatty tissue, and then eventually by fibrous scar tissue (cirrhosis).

FATTY LIVER

Most heavy drinkers have fatty livers, although they're unlikely to realise it because it hardly causes any symptoms at all – perhaps some dullness of appetite, or vague disturbance of the bowels. But the real worry about having a fatty liver is that there's a one-in-three risk it may quickly lead to cirrhosis – a very serious liver disease, more of which anon.

Fortunately, as long as this hasn't yet happened, and no other damage has been done, a fatty liver will recover completely if its owner cuts down on drinking.

ALCOHOL-INDUCED HEPATITIS

This is an inflammation of the liver that is brought on by a regular habit of heavy drinking. Its symptoms can be anything from little more than a mild discomfort in the right side and a listless 'liverish' feeling, to a serious, or even fatal, state of affairs in which the liver swells up, oozing fluid into the abdominal cavity, causing a hugely bloated belly, deep yellow jaundice and a risk of vomiting large amounts of bright red blood from engorged blood vessels in the gullet.

It appears that, in many people, alcohol seems to have the strange effect of forcing the liver cells to release antigens, which in turn stimulate the body's immune system to start attacking liver tissue, causing inflammation – alcohol-induced hepatitis. Fortunately, only a minority of heavy drinkers get this condition in its ghastly extreme form. But the milder form, with the listlessness and discomfort, is surprisingly common and often goes completely undiagnosed. The only clue may be high levels of liver enzymes in the blood, discovered by doing a special blood test.

For reasons not fully understood, women are more susceptible to alcohol-induced hepatitis than men. Their liver cells are more prone to release the auto-immune antigens which trigger liver inflammation in response to alcohol, and so they are more likely to suffer the consequences.

CIRRHOSIS OF THE LIVER

Both fatty liver and alcohol-induced hepatitis can lead to cirrhosis. It really means a badly damaged and permanently scarred liver (the word 'cirrhosis' comes from the Greek for 'tawny' – a reference to the liver's abnormally fibrous texture and pale colour). The worse the cirrhosis, the more scarring there is, and the less functioning liver the drinker has remaining.

Liver cells have remarkable powers of compensation – a dogged

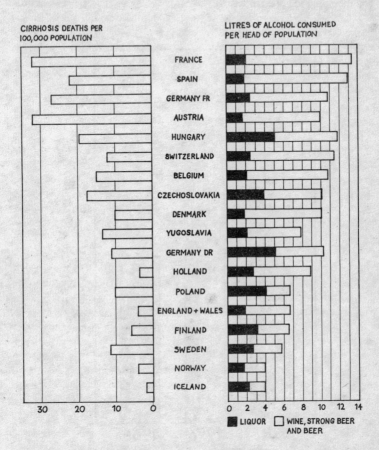

CIRRHOSIS DEATHS PER 100,000 POPULATION

LITRES OF ALCOHOL CONSUMED PER HEAD OF POPULATION

FRANCE
SPAIN
GERMANY FR
AUSTRIA
HUNGARY
SWITZERLAND
BELGIUM
CZECHOSLOVAKIA
DENMARK
YUGOSLAVIA
GERMANY DR
HOLLAND
POLAND
ENGLAND + WALES
FINLAND
SWEDEN
NORWAY
ICELAND

30 20 10 0

0 2 4 6 8 10 12 14

■ LIQUOR ☐ WINE, STRONG BEER AND BEER

persistence, soldiering on to the bitter end. If what's left is still in reasonable shape, then the person can survive for years. But if heavy drinking continues, and especially if hepatitis complicates the situation, then the liver, sooner or later, will be in dire straits. In the end there will be liver failure – with deep jaundice, a bloated abdomen, vomiting blood and, ultimately, terminal coma.

WILL YOUR LIVER LIVE A LITTLE LONGER? ....
With all these chronic liver problems, people vary greatly in the way they respond to them. It depends very much on whether your genes are 'right' or

The mounting toll of cirrhosis

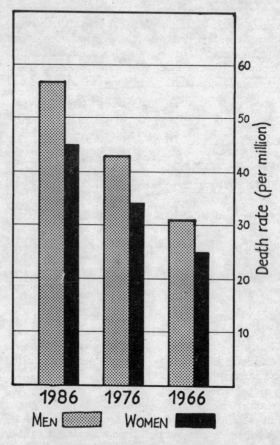

'wrong', how strong your constitution is, and how lucky or unlucky you are. For instance, black people are more at risk of cirrhosis than whites, because of a genetic susceptibility.

But by far the most important factor is how much you drink. For our typical 70kg (11st) man, drinking an average of 36–50 units a week (ie in the warning zone) puts up his risk of cirrhosis by six times that of a 'sensible' drinker. If he's drinking over 50 units a week (in the danger zone), his risk shoots up to at least 14 times normal. For a typical woman, the risks start mounting above 21 units.

According to the Royal College of Physicians, the majority of heavy drinkers will get fatty livers, and up to one in three will eventually get cirrhosis. The unfortunate thing is that most people don't notice any symptoms until the damage is all already well underway. And for any given level of tippling, there's no easy way of predicting who will run into trouble, and who will get away with it . . . or for how long.

But one thing you can be sure of. The less alcohol you drink, the less likely you are to have any of these problems. And if you've already got them, the sooner you stop drinking, the better your chances of recovery.

STOMACH
....

With every gulp of your drink, your oesophagus (gullet) conveys the alcohol to your stomach, and although it's only in contact with the booze for a few seconds at a time, this can be enough to cause the oesophagus a certain amount of irritation. Neat spirits are most likely to be a nuisance in this way, aggravating any heartburn you may be prone to, and giving you a constant feeling of wanting to burp away the discomfort in the middle of your chest.

Heavy spirit drinkers increase their risk of getting cancer of the oesophagus by about 20-fold. This is a rare but very nasty cancer, with a five-year survival rate of only one in 20. Oddly enough, for reasons we can't explain, smoking cigarettes adds to the drinker's risk of getting oesophageal cancer – doubling it by smoking 20 a day.

The stomach, too, comes in for a bashing with booze, again especially if you're drinking lots of spirits. A heavy bout on the bottle can irritate the stomach lining, causing gastritis, making you feel distinctly queasy, and giving rise to bilious indigestion. Not surprisingly, this kills off the appetite fairly effectively and, if it goes on for long enough, can lead to all sorts of problems caused by an inadequate diet. Chronic gastritis is the main cause of the debilitating malnutrition suffered by many alcoholics. Their stomach is literally pickled stiff – known by pathologists as 'leather-bottle stomach'. The acute gastritis suffered by those who indulge in occasional heavy drinking usually clears up completely within a day or two of moderation.

Although there is no evidence that alcohol can cause a peptic ulcer it almost certainly irritates the condition and slows down healing.

The pancreas, the organ responsible for producing digestive juices and insulin, may also be damaged by years of hard drinking. Chronic pancreatitis, a grumbling inflammation of the pancreas, is fortunately rare, but is increasing as more and more people take to long-term drinking. It causes severe bouts of upper abdominal pain, diarrhoea, malnutrition and, in some case, diabetes. Half its victims die within five years.

THE PROBLEM OF THE HEART

There's a widespread and fondly held belief that moderate drinking, say one or two units a day, is good for the heart. The idea is that somehow, perhaps by easing the effect of stress, or opening up the narrowed coronary arteries, it protects the heart from angina and heart attacks.

Unfortunately, this comforting thought (and wonderful excuse) is not borne out by evidence gathered in this country. Professor Gerry Shaper and his team at the Royal Free School of Medicine in London have reported on a long-term study of nearly 8000 middle-aged men in 24 towns throughout Britain, in which they found no significant link between the amount the men were drinking and their risk of heart disease. In other words, no evidence of any protection.

Although the light drinkers in Professor Shaper's study did indeed

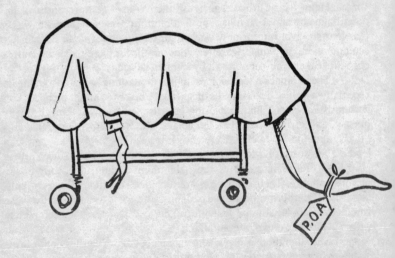

have a lower heart attack rate than the non-drinkers (and other studies around the world have also found this link), Professor Shaper pointed out that this finding might simply be a reflection of the fact that the sort of person who drinks lightly is usually also the sort of person who doesn't smoke, eats sensibly, takes exercise, and does all those other things that help to fend off heart trouble – and so may have nothing to do with alcohol at all.

In his report in the *British Medical Journal* Professor Shaper concluded: 'We should be extremely cautious about suggesting that regular drinking has health promoting attributes, even though there is no evidence that light drinking carries any hazard to health. Continued support for the "protective effect" of moderate alcohol consumption should be based on stronger evidence than is at present available.'

Stronger evidence, however, may at last be with us. A very large study in the States, involving 85,000 men and women over a four-year period, which was carefully corrected for such confounding influences as smoking habits, coffee drinking, and educational level, has found a significantly lower risk of heart disease among those who take one or two drinks a day compared with non-drinkers. Professor Shaper agrees that these new findings are indeed striking, and deserve further analysis.

There's no doubt all all, however, that very heavy drinking can damage the heart by causing fatty deposits in the heart muscle itself (cardiomyopathy) and disruption of the normal heartbeat rhythm (arrhythmia), but this is a fairly unusual side-effect of drink. Much more common, and fortunately only a temporary problem, is the alarming bout of severe palpitations (heart fluttering) that can come on the morning after a heavy night on the bottle – known in medical circles as the 'holiday heart syndrome'. Probably because doctors only do that kind of thing when they're away from home!

PUTTING ON THE PRESSURE

Every time you have a few drinks your blood pressure goes up a little – and then comes down again. This normal physiological response to the dilating effect of alcohol on skin capillaries has been known for many years. But only in the last decade have we discovered that alcohol is the commonest identifiable cause of long-term abnormally high blood pressure (hypertension).

The link was first noted among French soldiers during the First World War, but could never be confirmed. And it wasn't until several major research studies were recently undertaken, involving thousands of people, that the direct relationship between alcohol intake and blood pressure was fully appreciated. It seems to be clearly dose-related – the more you drink above the 'sensible' limit, the greater the risk of hypertension. Heavy drinkers treble the odds against themselves – and hence put up their likelihood of suffering the consequences of uncontrolled blood pressure: namely, a stroke, heart attack or kidney disease.

About one person in ten has high blood pressure severely enough to need medication with antihypertensive tablets. About one in three of these people are drinking to excess – twice as many as in those with normal blood pressure. This means that throughout Britain, nearly half a million people are having to take daily pills for a condition caused by drink. What's more, in many cases, the alcohol interferes with the medication, rendering it less effective.

STROKES

Heavy drinking also increases your risk of suffering a stroke – the destruction of part of the brain caused either by a clot in one of the cerebral arteries or by a haemorrhage. Very high doses of alcohol make the blood far more likely to form clots – and a heavy bout of drinking is one of the commonest causes of a stroke in a young person. Because long-term heavy drinking puts up the blood pressure, which can burst an artery in the brain, older people, too, have a higher risk of having a stroke if they drink heavily.

BURNING FEET

A burning discomfort or hypersensitivity in the feet is another common side-effect of chronic heavy drinking, affecting as many as one in ten of those people who seek medical help for their drinking, especially women. It's caused by a disturbance of the peripheral sensory nerves, and it's likely to be at least partly linked to a deficiency of B vitamins in the diet – most notably Vitamin B_1, or thiamine – heavy drinkers being particularly susceptible to a lack of this vitamin. The peripheral neuropathy, as the nerve disturbance is called, resembles a similar condition seen in certain cases of malnutrition in the Third World. This condition, also caused by thiamine deficiency, is known as beri-beri.

Lack of thiamine due to prolonged heavy drinking can also affect brain function, causing a state of confusion, apathy, disorientation and memory loss, together with unsteadiness and jerky eye movements, known as Wernicke-Korsakoff syndrome.

Both these forms of alcohol-induced thiamine deficiency are greatly helped by taking extra thiamine in multivitamin capsule form from the chemist's.

SATURDAY NIGHT PARALYSIS

This common problem can result from just one heavy drinking session. The drinker awakes from his semicomatose state to find that one arm is paralysed from the shoulder down, or that he can't move his foot. Known as 'Saturday Night Paralysis', it might be more appropriately called 'Sunday Morning Paralysis'.

What happens is that the drinker falls asleep in some awkward position – perhaps with his arm slung over the back of a chair, or his knee hard up against the wall – and in doing so squashes a nerve and paralyses it. It's a bit like your nerve going dead when you've been sitting awkwardly. Usually, you feel uncomfortable and shift position. But if you've been drinking heavily, you might be so deeply asleep that you are utterly oblivious to the nerve pressure, and the result could be a paralysis which persists for weeks – or might in rare cases even be permanent.

SEVEN DAYS DRINKING MAKE ONE WEAK

A prolonged bout of heavy drinking for several days can also give rise to severe aching and weakness in the muscles of the upper arms and legs. The drinker finds it difficult to stand or lift things (apart from another glass!), and just wants to slump in a chair. Biopsies (needle samples) of the affected muscles have shown that many of the microscopic muscles fibres have been destroyed by the alcohol.

Fortunately, except in older people (in this context those over the age of about 45), the muscle power fully recovers, with abstinence, after a few weeks. But in the meantime it could play havoc with your darts!

WITHDRAWAL SYMPTOMS

The classic picture of the alcoholic who can't get his 'fix' is a shaking, hallucinating, desperate wreck. Fortunately this condition is relatively rare. Far more common, although nowhere near as noticeable, are the minor symptoms of alcohol withdrawal among people who would never think of themselves as dependent on alcohol, but simply as social drinkers who like to have the occasional binge.

Twelve to 24 hours after the drinking bout, the person becomes extremely jumpy and restless. They are agitated and can't sleep. But their most striking symptom is 'the shakes' – a trembling of the hands. In severe cases they may get 'DTs' – delirium tremens – which leaves them confused, disorientated and experiencing hallucinations, often horrific in nature. These symptoms are very similar to those of a bad LSD trip, and may have a similar neurochemical cause – alcohol withdrawal stimulating the same or similar neurotransmitter chemicals in the brain as the hallucinogen.

MEN, SEX AND ALCOHOL

These three have long had a great thing going with each other. That is, apart from the well-known embarrassment of the great thing all-too-often becoming a rather small thing!

It would be remiss of me not to quote the immortal lines from Shakespeare's *Macbeth*:

'Lechery, sir, it provokes, and unprovokes; it provokes the desire, but it takes away the performance.'

Act II, Scene iii

And it's a theme not beneath the dignity of the health educators:

'There's one part any *beer can reach.'*
Health Education Council (after Heineken)

'Be hard – have a soft drink.'
Drinkwise North West Campaign

But, although brewers' droop is the butt of many a stand-up comic's routine, it can actually be the cause of a great deal of misery. Not so much because it's so often a bit of an anticlimax – the disappointing end to a riotous evening's debauchery – but because persistent heavy drinking can lead to long-lasting sexual difficulties.

Alcohol has a direct toxic effect on the testicles. It injures the cells that produce sperm, and also those responsible for the production of the male sex hormone – testosterone. And to add insult to injury, it damages the nerve pathways and hormonal links between the brain's sexual arousal centre, in the hypothalamus, and the pituitary gland, which controls the activity of the testicles. This means that persistently heavily drinking men have a number of problems caused by a lack of testosterone, and an overproduction of female sex hormones.

According to Dr Marsha Morgan, an alcohol expert at the Royal Free Hospital, London, a typical heavy drinker can become completely impotent, lose his libido (sexual urge), get shrinkage of his testicles and penis, suffer a major drop in his sperm count, lose his pubic hair, and get gross wrinkling of his scrotum.

The results of her researches hit the headlines in 1982:

'Drink'll wrinkle your winkle!'

Headline in The *Sun*

Men vary considerably as to how susceptible they are to this onslaught. But among very heavy drinkers (that's more than 50 units a week) seeking medical advice, the loss of libido is reported to range from 40–90 per cent depending on the degree of over-indulgence, and testicular shrinking from 10–75 per cent. About 40 per cent of men attending an infertility clinic were considered to have an alcohol-related low sperm count (too few and too immobile), drinking as little as four to six units daily (say, two or three pints).

Can all this devastation be reversed? I hear you cry.

Well, some of it can, in some cases. About 50 per cent of the infertile men returned to normal sperm production within three months of abstinence. And up to half of men with impotence find it improves if they stop drinking – providing their testicles haven't shrunk too small, and their pituitary gland still responds. But the Royal College of Physicians has stated that, for men with gross testicular shrinkage and inadequate sex hormone responses, very little can be done to help them.

So, lads, don't be fooled by the adman's image of the extra-strong lager-swiller's ultra-macho lifestyle. The real reason why he couldn't give a XXXX is because he can't.

CHAPTER NINE

A WOMAN'S LOT

---

*'After four large gins, my husband turns into a
disgusting beast. After five, I pass out altogether.'*

ANON

Over 90 per cent of women drink within the sensible limit recommended
by the Royal College of Physicians (14 units of alcohol a week; eg two
glasses of wine a day). But doctors are becoming increasingly concerned
at the growing number of heavy drinkers among younger women.

A recent nationwide study estimated that there are about 50,000
women under 30 drinking more than an average of five units a day. That's
well over double the sensible limit, and easily enough to seriously damage
their health. According to the OPCS (the government-funded Office of
Population Censuses and Surveys) about half of all those women who are
classified as 'heavy drinkers' (26 or more units a week) are under the age
of 25 and unmarried.

This is all very worrying because, although the overall figures for
women show no great increase in consumption, there does seem to be a
real epidemic of boozing among young women and girls, and this is now
beginning to show itself in other, even uglier, statistics:

- During the last ten years, the number of women caught over the
  legal limit for driving has doubled. For men, the conviction rate is
  up by only half as much again.
- Women have had to face a 22 per cent rise in the number of cautions
  for drunkenness over a decade. For men it was just 3 per cent.
- The past ten years have also seen an increase in the number of
  people being admitted to mental illness hospitals for treatment for
  alcohol misuse; again, relatively more women than men – about 25
  per cent compared with 20 per cent – and an increasing number of
  younger women.

- Women are particularly susceptible to chronic liver disease and cirrhosis caused by alcohol. Over the past decade, the number of women dying from these conditions has rocketed by about 20 per cent. Among men deaths are up by 15 per cent.
- All in all, about one woman in 12 is in serious trouble through drinking – and more and more problem drinkers are likely to be younger women.

THE RISKS TO HEALTH

The inescapable fact is that women are much more vulnerable than men to the effects of alcohol – not just the immediate intoxication, but more importantly, the insidious long-term permanent damage it causes them. In particular, the more alcohol women consume, and the longer they've been drinking, the more they risk chronic liver disease, such as cirrhosis – hence the special concern about the new younger drinkers. And if they're pregnant, or about to be, alcohol can carry a hazard for their baby too.

IMMEDIATE EFFECTS

We've already seen how women tend to get drunk faster than men, on the same amount of alcohol (*see* p.50). They also become more intoxicated. This is because these effects depend on the level of alcohol in the brain, which in turn depends on the level in the bloodstream (the blood alcohol concentration or BAC).

Women, being smaller on average than men, have less 'body room' in which to disperse that alcohol, and in particular have a smaller volume of blood in their circulation. Hence any given amount of alcohol will be more concentrated in a woman, and so will reach a higher BAC. The smaller the woman, the higher will be the BAC for any particular amount of drink.

'My mummy's favourite drink is a gin and panic.'
JESSICA, aged five

Women are also, on average, relatively plumper than men. They have a higher proportion of bodyfat in relation to muscle tissue. Because alcohol dissolves in water, but not in fat, it has even less room to take up – essentially just the blood, brain, heart, liver, other organs and the muscles. This means that, even if they're the same height and weight, a woman's BAC will usually be higher than a man's, for any given amount of alcohol.

LONG-TERM DAMAGE

Needless to say, women who drink heavily risk the same sorts of lasting damage to the brain, nervous system, liver, heart and other tissues as men. But as far as some long-term problems are concerned, notably those associated with the liver, they are very much more susceptible.

FATTY LIVER

Because women tend to have higher BACs than men, their poor old livers (or, increasingly, poor young livers) have to cope with a higher concentration of alcohol for any given amount of alcohol consumed. The result is that women's livers are much more likely to get fatty degeneration (*see* p.72). In fact, recent research in Toronto has shown that women drinking an average of 14–21 units a week multiply their risk of fatty liver by three times, compared with those who keep their consumption below 14. And above 21 units a week, the risk rises exponentially.

ALCOHOL-INDUCED HEPATITIS

This inflammation of the liver (described on p.72) is potentially fatal and seems to be triggered in many cases by an 'auto-immune' reaction. This means that the body's natural (and vital) defence system turns against its own tissue and starts attacking cells, causing inflammation. A number of common diseases are thought to be 'auto-immune' reactions – rheumatoid arthritis and mature-onset diabetes being the main examples. Scientists believe that some, as yet unidentified, agent triggers off these reactions. With alcohol-induced hepatitis, the liver comes under attack. And it's not just a straight toxic effect of alcohol, because it can happen with relatively low doses. It seems as though the alcohol acts as the trigger for the reaction in susceptible people. Again, for reasons unknown, women are more susceptible than men to auto-immune diseases, including alcohol-induced hepatitis. Some evidence suggests their risk is doubled.

CIRRHOSIS

For any given level of consumption, women are much more likely to get cirrhosis of the liver (*see* p.73), and the increase in the number of women, even young women, with this dangerous condition, is very worrying. Both fatty liver and alcohol-induced hepatitis are important predisposing factors, and the risk of these liver problems starts to mount up if you drink more than two units a day. At three units a day, the risk has tripled. Over five units a day (more than 35 a week) it's multiplied by about ten times.

We are all starting our drinking careers earlier in life, with parents allowing their children to quaff beer or sip wine at ever more tender ages (it's actually illegal to give a child under the age of five an alcoholic drink). A 1987 survey of 18,000 British schoolchildren revealed that 39 per cent of girls are regular drinkers, at least once a week, by the age of 11. This compares with 58 per cent of boys.

EFFECTS ON SEX ORGANS

Most of us know only too well how alcohol can so often provoke sexual excitement, closely followed by a rather embarrassing sexual disappointment. But few women realise that regular heavy drinking can detract from the enjoyment of sex in a more sinister way – by permanently damaging their ovaries, and hastening their menopause.

Alcohol not only has a direct toxic effect on the ovaries, reducing their output of female sex hormones (oestrogens), but can also depress the hypothalamus in the brain, and the pituitary gland linked to it. These last two places are where gonadotrophins are produced – the hormones that stimulate the ovaries into the right action at the right time.

All this means that persistent heavy drinking can upset normal sexual functioning in two main ways. Firstly, the lack of oestrogens makes the drinker more and more 'de-feminised'. The ovaries, breasts and sexual organs literally shrink. And the vagina becomes dry, making sex both difficult and painful. These changes are surprisingly common, even in younger women – about three out of four heavy drinkers noticing some loss of breast size, for instance.

Secondly, the interference with the normal sequence of gonado-trophins leads to irregular periods – some with heavy loss, others with no loss at all. And after several years of heaving drinking, the cycle can be completely disrupted, bringing on what is, in effect, a premature menopause.

As you can imagine, all this can be very upsetting for a woman, and her partner. Unfortunately, we don't know for certain what level of drinking is likely to cause these devastating effects – but similar effects in men happen with as few as five units a day, which is equivalent to about three and a half units a day for a woman.

Neither do we know whether any damage can be reversed by cutting down the drink. Again, information from studies of the similar damage to sexual function in men shows that once the testicles demonstrate signs of shrinkage, recovery is unlikely. It's likely that the same will be true for the ovaries and other organs in women.

DRINKING IN PREGNANCY

During pregnancy, alcohol, in common with many other drugs, can pass easily from the mother's bloodstream, through the placenta, into the developing embryo or fetus. Once there, depending on the amount of alcohol, and the stage of the pregnancy, it can do various sorts of mischief to threaten the unborn child.

HEAVY DRINKING

There's absolutely no doubt that heavy drinking can seriously change your baby's health by interfering with its genetic make-up, organ formation or physical and mental development before and after birth.

GENETIC MAKE-UP

There's evidence that, in the few days before conception, alcohol in high doses can alter the chromosomes of the ovum (egg), which hold the mother's contribution to the genetic code of the offspring. And studies have also shown that, for a week or two after conception, it can disrupt the chromosomes of the developing embryo. In other words, it's likely that a heavy drinking binge just before or after (or indeed during!) conception can induce chromosomal abnormalities, severely altering the genetic make-up of the embryo. This is likely to explain the increased risk of infertility and miscarriage experienced by women who are habitually heavy drinkers, *even if they cut out alcohol as soon as they know they're pregnant*.

The usual fate of an embryo with a major chromosomal abnormality is miscarriage at the time of the first, second or third 'missed period'.

ORGAN FORMATION

This occurs mainly in the third and fourth weeks after conception, with more detailed development during the following month or two. Again, alcohol can interfere with the process, causing structural abnormalities. If these are gross, the pregnancy is likely to be lost.

According to the Royal College of Physicians, women drinking as little as one or two units of alcohol a day in the first three months of pregnancy appear twice as likely as non-drinkers to have a miscarriage between the twelfth and twenty-fourth weeks.

THE NEWBORN BABY

There have been many research studies around the world, all of which show clearly that very heavy drinking during pregnancy can cause 'fetal alcohol syndrome'.

This is a horrific combination of abnormalities affecting the unborn baby, that can either result in a miscarriage, a stillbirth, or, most tragic of all, a child born with all sorts of congenital problems, including mental and physical retardation. These children are born small and fail to catch up with their growth. They have small heads, with a distinctive pug-faced appearance, and they have a number of major brain abnormalities. Their average IQ is about 70 (mental handicap of mild to

moderate severity) and they are prone to a variety of neurological problems, such as epilepsy, spasticity and clumsiness. They also tend to have
heart defects and various other internal abnormalities. Needless to say,
their prospects are not very bright.

'Very heavy drinking' in pregnancy usually means about ten
drinks *a day* – a level which only a very few mothers could keep up,
essentially those with a major drink problem – but even so they may still
go on to have an apparently healthy baby, although their chances of doing
so are greatly diminished. We simply don't know why some mothers have
affected babies and others don't.

> **'In terms of numbers affected, alcohol may be a
> vastly bigger problem for the unborn baby than
> thalidomide ever was.'**
> Professor Matthew Kaufman, Edinburgh University

But the worry is that it's likely that half that level of consumption
may sometimes give rise to some of the effects of fetal alcohol damage,
albeit not the full-blown syndrome. For instance, there may be some
minor abnormalities or learning difficulties, or perhaps growth retardation. Although a link with these relatively common problems can never
really be proved, many doctors are convinced that a pregnant woman
drinking about 35 or more units of alcohol a week (five a day) is taking a
big chance with her baby's future.

MODERATE DRINKING

But what about more moderate levels of drinking? What effect could they
have on the unborn child?

That question has proved to be extraordinarily difficult to answer
– so many other things impinge on the health of a fetus or baby, such as
the mother's nutritional state, smoking habits, drug or medication use,
and family income. Again, many studies have looked into it – but the
results have been conflicting. Some studies have shown that fairly low
consumption can have an adverse effect on such things as the risk of
miscarriage, stillbirth, having a premature baby, a small baby, or a baby
who has breathing difficulties. Other studies have not found the same
risks.

So, what does a conscientious mother-to-be do about it?
Obviously, the safest thing is not to drink any alcohol at all during

pregnancy – and indeed nearly half the women who become pregnant do stop altogether by about the third or fourth month. But the rest find complete abstention to be a bit too draconian for them, and want to know where to draw the line.

Some useful guidance on that score has recently come from Scotland. In a recent study involving nearly 1000 first-time mothers in Dundee, alcohol consumption of ten or more units a week was linked to an increased risk of having a smaller baby, and consumption of 12 or more units a week to having a premature baby more susceptible to breathing difficulties at birth. This was found to be true even after taking the mothers' smoking habits into account. Heavy drinking was quite clearly linked to having a smaller and more vulnerable baby.

The researchers concluded that if a mother-to-be continues to drink during pregnancy, she should make sure she keeps her consumption to less than ten units a week.

SOME SIMPLE GUIDELINES

So, what are the best guidelines for women who enjoy a drink, but want to guard against the downside of alcohol? The charitable organisation Alcohol Concern, an invaluable source of information and advice, offers the following:

- Be moderate with alcohol at all times – always avoid binge drinking.
- Aim for no more than two or three units of alcohol, two or three times a week.
- Have two or three alcohol-free days each week.
- Remember that above 14 units a week you're creeping into the danger zone.
- Cut down if you're drinking over 21 units a week. Contact Alcohol Concern (address at the back of this book), your GP, or any local alcohol advice agency if you're at all worried about your drinking. Don't delay in asking for help.
- Take special care if you're pregnant, or are planning to be. It's best to avoid alcohol at these times.

And I would add to this this last piece of advice – if you do continue to drink during pregnancy, keep below ten units a week.

STARTING YOUNG

It's easy to get the impression that the Italians and French have got it right, that their children are weaned on wine, and that Mediterranean family life is all the more wholesome for being firmly rooted in the communal open-air meal, replete with seafood and a never-ending flow of good cheap plonk, which adoring grandmamas pass around their little ones like a sacrament to kinship.

It's also natural to feel that we in Britain have an unnecessarily puritanical horror of the corrupting influence of alcohol on our children, and are only just beginning to emerge from the dark ages of fanatical Victorian temperance.

Both views are extreme and inaccurate. The Italians and French are careful to ensure that their children's drinking is little more than a few token sips. And surveys in this country show a surprisingly high level of alcohol consumption among children, from tinies tippling Dad's lager as he watches the football on the telly, to teenagers raiding the drinks cupboard or brass-necking it in the pub.

Experts in the alcohol field are especially worried about under-age drinking, partly because it's likely to set the pattern for boozing later in life, partly because children get drunk very easily indeed and do all sorts of mad and dangerous things, and partly because alcohol spells long-term health risks for youngsters.

'I started drinking in my teens, because that's what my friends did. Alcohol took away a lot of the inhibitions. I became more confident, a better conversationalist. In fact I believed people liked me better when I had a few drinks.'
　　　　　　　　　　　Alcoholics Anonymous member
　　　　　　　　　　　(quoted by Alcohol Concern)

In the previous chapter I looked at the problems associated with drinking at the time of conception, and during pregnancy, especially early on, and I described how alcohol can threaten the unborn baby. Now let's consider what drinking does to children themselves, either directly, or indirectly through their drinking parents.

Young children

One of the main worries with toddlers and the very young is that they are quite likely to guzzle drink in the same way that they might readily pop Dad's ulcer pills or Mum's tranquillizers. Adults often underestimate the ingenuity and dexterity of little ones in getting the top off some bottle or other, and taking a good draught of the contents. But whereas most parents will see to it that medicines are put safely away out of harm's reach, rarely is such care taken with the drinks cupboard. Casualty departments are all too familiar with some of the more severe effects of toddler intoxication – often dubbed the 'Sunday Morning Syndrome' – caused by plastered parents leaving half-empty bottles standing around for exploring young hands and mouths to find.

The smaller the child, the higher will be the blood alcohol concentration (BAC) for any given amount of drink. What's more, they can swallow a surprising quantity of alcohol while your back's turned. And thirdly, a child's little liver takes a lot longer to metabolize the stuff than does an adult's.

> 'I first started drinking at the age of seven when I found a bottle of sherry that my mother had won in a raffle, drank it, threw up, was out cold for about a day and wasn't forgiven easily by my Mum.'
>
> SIMON BATES

So, problems can arise very quickly. And with pre-school children can be extremely dangerous:

FACT: Small children who are severely intoxicated run the risk of getting hypothermia – a dangerously low body temperature – because the alcohol interferes with their internal thermostat.

FACT: They are also at risk of suffering from respiratory depression –

slow shallow breathing – because a relatively small amount of alcohol can anaesthetise the vital respiratory control centre in the brain.

FACT: Some toddlers are especially vulnerable to a sudden slump in their blood sugar level – hypoglycaemia – caused by swallowing alcohol. This can trigger epileptic-type fits, and is potentially life-threatening.

Seven- to ten-year-olds

Older children who experiment with drink – usually by sneaking bottles from their parents drinks-cabinet and sharing it with their pals down the street – often end up in casualty as accident victims. Cuts, fractures, head injuries and hypothermia are the most common problems. The children – boys more than girls – often find themselves unable to get home from their drinking den without injury, or are found, hours later, staggering or semicomatose, and frozen to the marrow.

Teenage drinking

Style. Seductiveness. Sophistication. Speed. Sensation. All the 'S' words that spell excitement and sex. These are the themes of so much drinks advertising aimed at what the creative directors call the 'fresh flesh' end of the market. In music papers, cinemas and pop videos co-sponsored by

drinks companies, the message rings out to aware, eager young people. Join the set. Drink to your dreams.

Small wonder then that teenage drinking has never before reached such a peak, and that there's hardly a pub, school, or court in the land that hasn't seen more than its share of problems caused by youngsters taking the bottle and the law into their own hands.

But just how much teenage drinking is really going on? And is it really such a terrible scourge? Or more an epidemic of over-reaction by the usual reactionaries?

Paragon of health virtue, Edwina Currie, admits that she started young on lager-and-lime. As a teenager she'd tell her mother she was going to the Wavertree Coffee House. 'It sounded innocent enough,' she recalls. 'But in fact it's one of the biggest pubs in Liverpool.'

A recent study of young people's behaviour helps to answer these questions. No fewer than 18,000 schoolchildren aged 11–16 in 600 British schools were surveyed in 1987 by Dr John Balding of the Health Education Authority's Schools Health Education Unit, University of Exeter. The survey found that:

- 50 per cent of 11-year-olds had drunk alcohol at least once in the previous seven days
- that's 60 per cent of 11-year-old boys, and 40 per cent of 11-year-old girls
- by the fifth year (15-year-olds) 50 per cent of boys had drunk five or more units during the week
- the equivalent figure for 15-year-old girls was 30 per cent.

But the really worrying result was that concerning safe levels of drinking. You'll remember that for men of average build the maximum sensible level is 21 units a week, and for women, 14. You'll probably also recall that these levels should be revised downwards for slimmer people and relatively inexperienced drinkers. Well, Dr Balding's 'Young People in 1987' study found that no fewer than 10 per cent of 15-year-old boys were exceeding the sensible level for drinking, and about 5 per cent of girls.

'Young people are less experienced drinkers, they
are also bigger risk-takers in general. They tend
to think "what the hell?" about a lot of things,
alcohol makes you think "what the hell?" even
more – combine the two and you have a big
increase in risk-taking; that's why accidents
among young people are so high . . . I saw a young
man last week in Glasgow who had had a few
pints of beer, went home, fell down the stairs,
wasn't discovered until morning, and who is now
permanently brain-damaged. But there are other
risks as well if you drink too much and you're
young: drugs, AIDS, sexual dangers for young
women – you're more liable to be pressurised into
things you wouldn't normally do when you've had
too much to drink.'

Dr Ian Robertson

The most popular drink among boys is beer or lager, with over half of
15-year-olds having at least a pint in the previous week. Over 10 per cent
admitted to an average of a pint a *day*. The girls' favourite tipple was
wine, one in three having at least one glass in the week. Spirits were most
popular with girls – about one in four having had at least a single in the
previous seven days, and over one in 20 having an average of one shot a
day.

Most 15-year-olds got their drink from home, with or without
parents' permission; and the next best source was the pub (the main
source for over 25 per cent of the youngsters). Discos and parties were the
other main places for drinking.

Great controversy surrounds the idea of issuing
identity cards to 18–25-year-olds. The National
Association of Licensed Victuallers has started a
voluntary card scheme, hoping its members
(mainly publicans) will offer these to bona fide
18-year-olds. Several schools have started similar
schemes. The Government is coming under
increasing pressure to institute a national scheme

....

– the idea being that local authorities could issue
the cards with voting forms. But civil liberties
groups have long argued that such a system
would be a serious infringement of individual
rights to anonymity – carrying identity cards has
always seemed a shade too close to the horrors of
pass laws and a police state.

....

Compared with a previous report, the trend is rising. And yet a recent analysis of drunkenness offences by young people does not bear out the widely held view that teenage drinking poses a threat to society. According to the Home Office the number of boys caught drunk, about 4400 in 1987, has fallen in recent years. And the equivalent figure for girls, about 440, has remained stable. The rate of drunkenness among the under 18s is actually no higher than among those aged 30–60!

KIDS, BOOZE AND THE LAW
....

Licensing laws have undergone a few changes recently, but those relating to under-age drinking have remained substantially the same. Here are the basics . . .

UNDER FIVES ....
- It's against the law to give alcohol of any kind to a child under five – except on doctor's advice, or in a medical emergency when deemed necessary by a 'responsible person'.

UNDER 14s ....
- They aren't allowed in a bar during opening hours, *unless*:
  – they are just passing through
  – they are resident
  – they are children of the licensee.
- They are however allowed in a 'family room' or pub garden provided it's quite separate from any bar, and there is no direct drinks service to it.

UNDER 16s

- In a restaurant or eating area, they may be allowed to drink alcohol with their meal, if purchased by an accompanying adult.
- They are *not* allowed to buy it themselves.

14–18s

- They may be allowed into a bar at the licensee's discretion, *but* mustn't drink alcohol there, nor be sold it.
- In a licensed restaurant or eating area, 16–17-year-olds may buy beer, cider or perry to drink with their meal, but not wine or spirits.
- They may however drink wine or spirits with their meal if these are purchased by an accompanying adult.
- In Scotland, 16–17-year-olds may buy and consume beer, cider, perry *and wine*, with their meal.

ALL UNDER 18s

- They mustn't buy or drink alcohol at a bar in any pub, wine bar, disco, hotel, airport, station or other bar-type premises.
- Anyone who tries to buy an alcoholic drink for someone under 18 in a bar is committing an offence.
- Any bar licensee who sells alcohol to someone under 18, knowingly or unknowingly, has committed an offence; unless they can demonstrate that they tried their best to check the age. The fine has recently been quadrupled to £400.
- In Northern Ireland no one under 18 can enter licensed premises without breaking the law, unless they are resident, or children of the licensee.
- Under 18s may enter off-licences (including the off-licence area of supermarkets or grocers), but are not allowed to buy alcohol. Any off-licensee selling alcohol, knowingly or unknowingly, to someone under 18 is liable to prosecution, unless they can demonstrate that they tried their best to check the age.
- Under 18s may not work in a bar during opening hours, even without payment, and even if they are the licensee's children.

. . . You have been warned!

CHAPTER ELEVEN

HIGH SOCIETY?

We drink for the pleasure it gives. We drink for companionship. We drink to celebrate. We drink to relax. We drink to get to know people. And we drink to each other's health and happiness.

What a sad irony it is then that that same drinking, which helps to bring so much joy, well-being and friendship into our lives, is also the catalyst of so much ill-feeling, misery and cruelty. Quite apart from the direct physical harm that alcohol can have on our bodies, it also plays a colossal part in the disruption and destruction of our society.

The flip-side of alcohol can be seen everywhere – on the streets, in the terraces, in the courts, in casualty departments, in broken homes, and wrecked careers.

Our high society comes at a high cost.

ON THE HOME FRONT

Family life can be affected by excessive drinking in a number of ways. For one thing, a heavy drinking habit is likely to undermine the family's economic security, both as a drain on financial resources and as a potential cause of job-loss. Drinkers often get into serious debt, living on plastic money or deferred bills, and taking their mind off how they're going to pay for it all by pouring themselves another drink. Forty per cent of family social work cases cite alcohol as a contributory factor.

Rows and acts of violence in the home, whether between husband and wife or parent and child, are frequently related to alcohol. A third of heavy drinkers reckon there is a link between their alcohol problems and marriage difficulties. A recent survey of 100 battered wives revealed that 52 of their husbands were 'frequently drunk', and with another 22 there had been periods of 'heavy drinking and drunkenness'.

But no amount of statistics can describe what it is like to live under the same roof as someone with an alcohol problem. Violence needn't be a factor. Suspicion, doubt and fear cause their own tensions and leave their

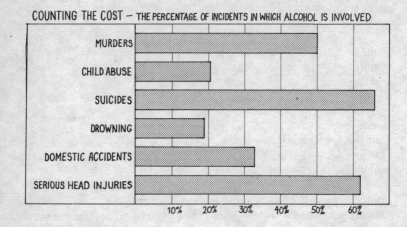

COUNTING THE COST — THE PERCENTAGE OF INCIDENTS IN WHICH ALCOHOL IS INVOLVED

own scars. The words of a caring, watchful spouse can easily be twisted by the problem drinker into yet another example of nagging interference – and the drinker may well reassert his or her own will by drinking more.

If the couple have children, they too are bound to be affected. Physical and verbal abuse are not the only problems. A child may also suffer from neglect if one or both parents are totally bound up in their drink problems. Psychiatric illness, juvenile delinquency and, in the end, their own problems with alcohol have a six times higher than average incidence amongst children of heavy drinkers.

TEACHER: *How's your baby brother?*
JULIE (aged 5): *He's in hospital.*
TEACHER: *Oh dear. Why?*
JULIE: *Daddy stabbed him with a fork.*
TEACHER: *Why did he do that?*
JULIE: *He was drunk.*
Conversation between a primary school teacher and one of her pupils. Julie is not her real name.

It has been estimated that two out of three suicides, and nearly as many attempted suicides, are committed by people who have been drinking. Heavy drinkers account for about a third of that total. As alcohol promotes a devil-may-care recklessness in us, so it increases the chances that a suicide attempt – which may start out as no more than an attention-seeking 'cry for help' – will result in death.

About 6000 deaths and 2 million injuries are the result of accidents in the home, and roughly a third of these are associated with alcohol. The majority of these accidents involve falls (due to impaired co-ordination and sluggish reaction times) and complications with drugs – overdoses and ill-advised mixtures which are often down to drunken carelessness. A glass of wine in the kitchen may be a legitimate perk for a busy cook, but it doesn't pay to get overcasual with the vegetable knife or slapdash when frying – nasty cuts and chip-pan fires happen often enough to sober cooks. The living-room offers more fire hazards – alcohol, cigarettes and inflam-mable furniture materials can be a deadly combination; not only is a fire more likely to be started by a soporific smoker, the same person is not going to be in any state to put the fire out or make an escape. Forty per cent of domestic fires are linked to excessive drinking.

We get a lot of accidents in the home due to alcohol, where people have put a chip-pan on the stove and they have been having a drink and they forget about it, or they fall asleep, or people don't stub out their cigarettes . . . Housefires are often caused through alcohol. Also people tend to lose their inhibitions when they've had alcohol, and we get a lot of domestic rows and a lot of domestic assaults through alcohol.

Casualty nurse

TROUBLE AT WORK

You don't need to drink at all to appreciate that Monday mornings are an especially common time for absenteeism. But for the heavy drinker the effects of too much alcohol make the weekly return to work even harder to stomach. Between 8 and 14 million working days are lost each year because of heavy drinking. Less regular drinkers will also take the occasional liberty in order to nurse themselves through a hangover. In a 1987 survey of drinking patterns, 10 per cent of the men questioned admitted that drink had, at some time or other, had a detrimental effect on their work. Whether someone with a hangover is of more use (and less harm) to their company by staying at home or coming to work is open to question. Three-quarters of problem drinkers are in employment – and about 5 per cent of working men and 1 per cent of working women have a drink problem.

Not surprisingly, drinkers have more accidents at work and, if they are working with heavy machines the results can be fatal. Those without a specific drinking problem may also endanger themselves and others by handling dangerous equipment after a 'liquid lunch', when it takes only a couple of beers to seriously diminish a worker's capabilities and reaction times. It's reckoned that at least one in five of all accidents at work are linked to drink, usually occurring at the start of a shift or just after lunch. For this reason, alcohol is strictly deterred in many occupations, and banned on oil-rigs.

'You wouldn't want a fireman's lift off one of us after we've had a couple of pints.'

Fireman

But mixing drink with work is by no means a problem unique to the machine operator or manual labourer. Management decisions clouded by alcohol may lead to economic difficulties and redundancies which, though not quite so fatal, may nonetheless be severely damaging to the employees' prospects.

All in all, what with the poor performance, lost production, accidents at work, absenteeism, and sick pay, the total bill that booze presents to British industry is well over £2 billion – a year.

Working colleagues tend to cover up for their mates rather than 'shop' them – but this may not always be in the problem drinker's best interests – it depends very much on the firm's policy and attitude. Many employers will summarily dismiss someone who is found to be 'a drinker', without a thought for sick leave, confidentiality, job security, pension rights or future employment prospects.

It's important for employers to identify those of their workforce who may have a drink problem and help them to get help for it. Safety, productivity and the fear of litigation are all powerful motives for employers to do something about it.

'Heavy losses are caused by excessive drinking, alcoholism, problem drinking, and that coupled with the safety hazards in a manufacturing situation means that there is room to have a co-ordinated, totally applied policy for all employees ... There is also the humanitarian aspect ... we do a great deal of good for both the employee and his family, and this motivates the people who work in GEC alcoholism schemes very much indeed.'

Bob Randall, GEC Alcohol Advisory Service

Ideally, once identified, the drinking employee should be offered some sort of counselling, with a mutually agreed target for tackling and overcoming the problem. If necessary, rehabilitation facilities should be provided by the employer, either in-house or via an outside agency. An understanding, rather than a threatening, approach should be adopted.

THE CRIMINAL STREAK

According to the majority of studies, about 50 per cent of all crimes are alcohol-related.

The great majority of offenders are male, and tend to be under 25. And the problem is by no means confined to the mean streets of the inner cities. A recent survey of market towns throughout England and Wales, picturesque paragons of gentility and rectitude, shows public disorder to be rife there, too, particularly among young people, and that 90 per cent of this vandalism, brawling and disturbance of the peace is drink-related. Several town councils are trying pilot schemes which ban drinking in public places in an effort to curb the alcoholic excesses of their unruly youngsters.

> *'If anybody still in this day and age is telling me that there's no link between alcohol and crime then I'm afraid that they just don't live in the real world. You only have to go into any police station . . . any battered wives refuge . . . any crisis centre . . .'*
>
> NICK ROSS

There is no doubt that alcohol encourages some people to take risks, and break rules. It also unleashes aggression. But how often does this lead to violent crime? After all, a few drinks too many doesn't turn everybody into a vicious thug. It is just as common to start finding bad jokes hilarious, burst into tears, pontificate on the meaning of life, or simply fall asleep. Our reaction to drink will depend on our personality, our mood at the time, and our situation. In seeking the cause of aggression, it is important to look at factors like these before we heap all the blame on alcohol.

'St Francis of Assisi wouldn't have headbutted someone after 12 pints of bitter, so you can't always say that alcohol causes crime, but some crimes simply wouldn't happen if people weren't very drunk; for instance after pub closing time . . . In Scotland alcohol was banned at football matches in the early 80s and there was a big drop in violence, so it must be a cause of some violence. It's also a rallying call, a symbol of aggression, and it lands an awful lot of people in trouble.'

Dr Ian Robertson

One famous experiment investigated the effect of different drinks on the behaviour of male medical students. The drinks were doctored so that some of the students received watered down spirits or beer, others had drinks that were laced with extra alcohol, and the drinks of others were quite normal. It was all done very subtly so that the guinea-pigs had no idea that anything was out of the ordinary, and the researchers themselves didn't know which drink was which until after the experiment was over.

The interesting finding was that the students who thought they were drinking most alcohol were more aggressive in the group than those who thought they were drinking least – *whether or not their true alcohol intake was high or low*.

Whitbreads have employed a behavioural psychologist to identify the factors that make some drinkers become aggressive and violent, and to train publicans in recognising the early signs of antisocial behaviour. It may seem that most publicans are fairly good at this already, but Whitbread's publicans will have the added experience of interpersonal skills training, group work and role play. And it's likely that other breweries won't be far behind in the appliance of science to the gentle art of bouncing.

Peer group pressure, it seems, sustains a macho culture amongst a large percentage of the male population, particularly in the 18–30 age group, and it is from this group that most of the perpetrators and victims of violence come. If you are looking for trouble, you are more than likely to find it. Anticipation of a fight fuels the mood of the evening. Drink oils the wheels, but it is not the starting point.

All the same, many acts of violence would not occur were it not for the lubricant of alcohol. As I've said, alcohol sheds inhibitions, excuses bad behaviour (in the drinker's mind – for a while, at least), and provides 'Dutch courage'. It also diminishes our rational faculties, making misunderstandings much more likely to occur; the arguments that spark off drunken brawls, and even murder, are often absurdly trivial.

Moving away from violent crime, studies show that more than 50 per cent of convicted burglars have been drinking prior to committing the offence. But there is a complication here, in that the figures refer only to those burglars who have been *caught*; clearly there can be no drinking statistics on the ones that got away. Since a burglar is more likely to escape detection by performing the job in a sober state, the true proportion of burglaries committed under the influence of alcohol may be a good deal under 50 per cent. But then again, many burglars (convicted or otherwise) would never have dreamt of committing their first offence were it not for the disinhibiting effect of alcohol and the tendency towards recklessness which it so often inspires.

VICTIMS

But what of the victims of crime? What part does alcohol play in their plight? A recent study in Bristol looked at nearly 500 victims of assault who had gone to the casualty department at the main city hospital. Researchers asked them about their alcohol intake over the previous 12 hours, and then compared the answers with the severity of the patients' injuries. As you might expect, the more drink they'd had, the worse were their injuries.

In the world's largest study of the link between alcohol consumption and cause of death in young men, researchers analysed the answers to a questionnaire completed by nearly 50,000 Swedish army conscripts, aged 18–19.

They showed a striking connection. Men who drank more than 25 units a week were twice as likely to die within 15 years than those who drank under ten units. The cause of death was mostly violent (75 per cent), and about half of those (and this may come as a surprise to you) were suicide. For reasons that are obscure, Sweden has a high suicide rate. Other violent deaths were road accidents, poisonings, drownings, falls, and murder/manslaughter, in that order.

RAPE

There have been many studies of the motivating factors in cases of rape, including the effect of alcohol. Information from urine samples, police files, testimonies and court evidence has been gathered on over 2000 rapists and other sex offenders, and a similar number of rape victims, mainly in the United States. Overall, about half the offenders had been drinking prior to the attack. Interestingly, a higher than expected proportion of the victims had also been drinking – particularly group-rape victims (41 per cent).

CHAPTER TWELVE

DRIVING v. DRINKING

It was a dull wet dreary Monday morning. Ten-year-old Louise was walking to school with her friends, chatting and larking about. A steady stream of cars was filing past into town. Without looking behind her, Louise suddenly stepped off the kerb.

Somehow the driver of the red Sierra didn't see her in time. He jammed on the brakes – skidded – and felt the sickening thud. Louise was thrown back on the pavement with multiple injuries, including a fractured skull.

The policeman noticed a whiff of something on the driver's breath. The breathalyser read 43 – equivalent to a blood alcohol concentration (BAC) of 95mg per 100ml. The legal limit for driving is a breathalyser reading of 35, and a BAC of 80.

At just after nine o'clock that morning, the driver made a statement at the police station – and Louise died in casualty.

Of all the ways in which alcohol can impinge on our lives, the wanton carnage of road accidents must be the most awful, and the most pathetic. The numbers involved are horrifying. I know many people find statistics a bore and a blur, but no one can ignore them:

- There are well over a quarter of a million road accidents every year in Britain – killing about 5500 people, and seriously injuring nearly twenty times that many.
- At least one in every four road accident deaths is linked to alcohol – nearly 1500 a year.
- Of those, up to 1000 are killed while driving over the legal limit for alcohol.
- And over 300 are pedestrians who have been drinking.
- The rest, like Louise, are 'innocent' victims of someone else's carelessness.

All in all, more people are killed by drink-drivers in Britain than are murdered. And more people are seriously injured by drink-drivers than are mugged or assaulted. Over the past decade that adds up to a horrifying 170,000 personal tragedies on our roads, associated with alcohol. Quite apart from the price in human misery, it's been reckoned that drink-driving costs the economy over £1,000,000 every *day* – in damage to vehicles and property, medical costs, court fees and police work, sick pay and lost production.

There are roughly 600 homicides each year in this country: that includes all categories of murder, manslaughter and infanticide. About ten times as many people are killed on the roads . . . Crime somehow captures our imagination. How many feature films are there about road accidents? How many novels that grip the imagination are there about drink-driving? But actually drink-driving is the issue that really ought to worry us most.'

NICK ROSS

And yet, all it takes to cause, or become, one of these ghastly statistics, is one drink too many. That one drink that takes us over the limit.

But surely, anyone who's used to drink, knows when they've had enough, don't they? They're not so daft as to drive when they're that drunk, are they? Any decent driver can handle a car even better after a few pints can't they?

'Having done a couple of programmes on killer drivers, the last one a month ago, where virtually the entire audience was composed of people who'd lost relatives killed by drunken drivers, no way I could ever now have even a touch of alcohol and drive a car.'

ROBERT KILROY-SILK

Well, actually . . . no. Alcohol slows your reactions, and interferes with your judgement of such crucial factors as speed, distance, and angles.

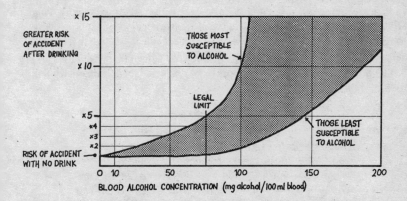

You're more easily distracted and less likely to heed warnings. You have more difficulty on strange roads, and get more easily bamboozled by unfamiliar roadworks. You're more likely to under-react, or over-react to hazards. In short, you're a liability, and perhaps a menace.

Well (I hear you protest), maybe after a skinful. But a few won't hurt surely?

Not so. These changes begin to happen within 30 minutes of your *first* drink. Although measurable, they are unlikely to be noticed by you or anyone else. But with each succeeding drink, your blood alcohol concentration (BAC) rises, your driving skills deteriorate, and your accident risk increases:

- At a BAC of 50mg% (two or three standard units), the average driver's risk of an accident is appreciably higher than it would be without drinking.
- At a BAC of 80 (the legal limit in the UK), it's roughly *double*.
- At a BAC of 120 (pleasantly merry), it zooms up to about *tenfold*.
- At a BAC of 160 (rather tiddly), it's approaching *25 times*

Younger people (under 25) and the elderly (over 70) have a relatively higher accident risk at these levels. Hardened drinkers, relatively lower.

To find out exactly how many drinks will give you these BACs, turn to p.58. As you'll see, it depends on your sex, weight and drinking history. If you're a women, if you're lighter than average, or if you're less of a drinker than most, it will take fewer drinks to make you more accident prone and take you over the limit.

One in every three drivers killed has a BAC of 80 or more. After closing time this rises to over half the drivers killed. And between 10pm and 4am on a Saturday night it averages three out of every four drink driver deaths. These percentages are even higher in Scotland.

And it certainly isn't just rotten luck – the occasional drinker who gets caught out. A recent Swedish survey has shown that about half of all alcohol-related crashes involve problem drinkers (regular heavy drinkers with some alcohol dependence).

'I think people who drink and drive should never get a second chance. They should never drive again. If somebody discharges a firearm or a shotgun irresponsibly, and especially if they were drunk, what would happen if they applied for a firearm certificate? Rightly they'll say, "You must be joking, get lost." A car is just as lethal.'

MARTIN SHAW

DRINKING, DRIVING AND THE LAW
....

It's been an offence to drive a vehicle 'under the influence' since the days of horse-drawn carriages. But, prior to the 1967 Road Safety Act, the evidence for conviction was based on the suspicion of a police officer, and an assessment by the police surgeon. Suspected drink-drivers had to undergo the indignity of trying to say, 'The Leith police dismisseth us', or 'Brian's back brake-block is broken'. They would have to pigeon-step along the chalk line, and stand stock still with their eyes shut without a hint of sway. As a confirmatory test, the police surgeon resorted to a blood or urine test.

POLICEMAN: *'Right sir. How many fingers am I holding up?'*
DRIVER: *'Eleven, officer.'*

Since 1967, however, the policeman's lot has been an easier one, thanks to the advent of the breathalyser. Originally, it was a tube or crystals which, if you had more than about 35 micrograms of alcohol per cent in your breath, changed colour as you blew through them into a bag. If the breathalyser result was suspicious, the driver would be required to offer a blood or urine sample at the station. If the equivalent blood alcohol level was above 80mg%, the driver was deemed to have committed an offence. The penalty on first conviction was to be banned from driving for a year and pay a fine.

POLICEMAN:	*'Would you please blow hard into this, sir.'*
DRIVER:	*'Certainly, officer.' (blows)*
POLICEMAN:	*'And this too, please, sir.'*
DRIVER:	*'Anything to oblige, officer.' (blows again)*
POLICEMAN:	*'Thank you, sir. These gloves are useless on a cold night.'*

The effect on accidents was dramatic. In the year after the introduction of the breathalyser and new penalties, serious road accidents fell by 11 per cent, and deaths by 15 per cent. Over the following seven years, about 5000 lives had been saved.

In 1983 a new improved electronic digital breathalyser was introduced which, in tandem with a confirmatory breathalyser at the station, is deemed sufficient evidence to secure conviction, and cuts out all the fiddling about with blood and urine samples. As a result, about 120,000 people a year are brought to book for drink-driving.

But that's still only a fraction of the numbers who are playing Russian roulette with their (and other people's) lives. Hence the call for stiffer penalties and random breath testing. A recent national survey by the Roadwise Campaign found 75 per cent of people in favour of a lower legal limit for driving, and nearly 80 per cent in favour of random breath testing.

The way the law stands at the moment, the police can only conduct a breath-test if they have reasonable cause to suspect a driver of:

- having committed a moving traffic offence
- having been involved in an accident

This considerably restricts their detection rate. In recent years, random testing has been introduced successfully in many parts of the world, including Scandinavia, Australia, New Zealand, and most of the USA. In Finland, for example, where it was launched in 1977, the drink-driving rate has halved.

LEGAL LIMITS FOR DRIVING

BAC	COUNTRY
0 mg% (no alcohol)	Bulgaria, India
20 mg%	Poland
50 mg%	Chile, Finland, Greece, Iceland, Japan, Netherlands, Norway, Portugal, Sweden, some states of the USA, Yugoslavia
50 or 80 mg%	Australia (depending on which state)
80 mg%	Austria, Belgium, Canada, Denmark, France, Luxembourg, New Zealand, Spain, Switzerland, United Kingdom, West Germany
100 or 150 mg%	Some states of the USA
120 mg%	Eire
No limit	Italy

The British Government has recently announced a tough new crackdown on drink-drivers. A new offence of 'causing death by careless driving while unfit through drink or drugs' will carry up to five years' imprisonment, disqualification for a minimum of two years, and an unlimited fine. Another new penalty of 'dangerous driving' will earn a maximum sentence of two years in jail. In general, courts will be able to rap drink-drivers much more severely, and anyone disqualified will have to pass a much tougher driving test to get their licence back. Some offenders will have to go on a rehabilitation course, and anyone with two convictions within ten years, or a BAC more than 200mg% (two and a half times the legal limit), will have to satisfy the authorities that they have managed to kick the booze habit before they'll be allowed to drive again. Separate proposals for random breath-testing are likely to be adopted shortly.

In my introduction to this book, I said it isn't anti-alcohol, and I've tried to present a balanced view. But if you get nothing else out of it, I do hope that at least you'll be able to work out when to stop drinking if you're driving. Needless to say, the safest thing is to either steer clear of alcohol completely, or stay low. And to help you with that, I've given a list of no-alcohol and low-alcohol beers, ciders and wines on pp.131–2.

PROBLEM? WHAT PROBLEM?

'An alcoholic is someone you don't like, who drinks as much as you do.'

DYLAN THOMAS

Several times in this book I've used the term 'problem drinker'. I've also talked about 'heavy drinkers', and I've frequently described people as being 'alcohol-dependent'. Very occasionally I've said 'alcoholic'.

But what exactly do these words mean? And what's the difference between them?

HEAVY DRINKERS

Let's take 'heavy drinker' to start with, because it has no meaning whatsoever. At least, there's no agreement as to how it should be defined. The Royal College of Physicians says one thing, the Royal College of Psychiatrists another. I prefer to go along with the Office of Population Censuses and Surveys, whose job it has been to actually count the number of drinkers at the various different degrees of indulgence. The OPCS defines two categories within the overall label 'heavy drinkers' – 'fairly heavy' and 'very heavy'. 'Fairly heavy' are those men who drink 36–50 units a week, and 'very heavy' those who drink more than 50. For women the equivalents are 26–35 units, and more than 35. Thus:

	MEN (units/ week)	% of adult pop'n	WOMEN (units/ week)	% of adult pop'n
Fairly heavy:	36–50	6	26–35	1
Very heavy:	over 50	6	over 35	1
All 'heavy':	over 35	12	over 25	2

Typical drinking careers

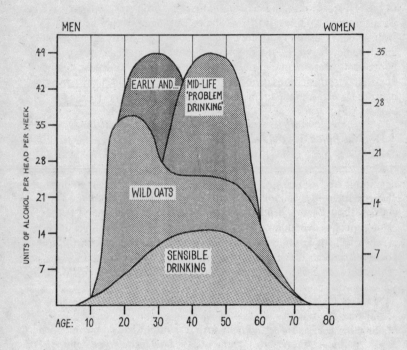

....

'**People who drink heavily are not just the lager louts and the down and outs: in fact they are in the minority, and most people who drink heavily are like you and me, they are perfectly normal people with jobs and families. They are often cocooned from the fact that they are heavy drinkers by the fact that most of their friends are heavy drinkers too.**'

Dr Ian Robertson

....

It follows from this that one in eight men, and one in 50 women, are 'heavy drinkers'. But among young people (18–24-year-olds), these proportions are much higher at nearly one in four young men, and one in 17 young women. Note also that 'fairly heavy' corresponds with the 'Warning Zone' for health risks, and 'very heavy' with the 'Danger Zone' (*see* p.24). Heavy drinking may therefore cause problems, especially if it is persistent and continues for some time. But many people go through a spell of heavy drinking without apparent ill-effect and without running into trouble. A typical drinking 'career' might be a period of hitting the booze pretty hard in one's youth – sowing wild oats – and then steadying up as the responsibilities of job and family take over. So, heavy drinking may not necessarily lead to 'problem drinking', but in many cases does.

PROBLEM DRINKING

Now let's turn to 'problem drinkers'. Again there's no hard and fast definition. And it's easy to see why, because really all it means is someone whose drinking causes problems. It may cause problems for themselves – perhaps hangovers, a drink-drive conviction, or liver trouble. Or it may cause problems for other people – perhaps rows with the spouse, slumping at work, a fight at the pub. Or usually both. There are an awful lot of possible problems that can be caused by drink, and I've spent an awful lot of this book describing them. It can interfere with your life, or the life of someone you know, all too easily.

But it's not always so easy for the problem drinker to realise or accept that drink is the cause of the problem – or is even adding to it. Making this link can be difficult:

- The middle manager who consistently under-performs at work, misses deadlines, loses the confidence of staff, and feels more and more bypassed and undervalued, may not be able to face the fact that much of his or her problem is drink.
- The mother of three children under five who is finding them more and more difficult, hit her eldest far too hard the other day, can never quite get things done, can't get out to the shops, and is completely off sex, and yet simply doesn't see that her only comfort is actually a major part of her troubles.
- The 23-year-old central-heating fitter who has just been done for driving over the limit, been banned for a year, and is now stuck with public transport, lost the girlfriend, and has his arm in a sling with a broken collar bone, but still spends nearly every evening getting canned down the local with his mates.

A problem drinker may not necessarily be a heavy drinker. It's obviously quite possible to have a drink-related problem, such as an accident at work or a hangover, or nothing more sinister than a more-than-usually liquid lunch or a rare four-pint binge. But most people who recognise that drinking is a recurring theme in their problems do in fact drink heavily.

And many of them feel they need help with coming to terms with, and doing something about, their drinking. They realise that their drinking isn't simply a cause of, or contributing factor to, their problem – it *is* their problem.

THE EARLY SIGNS OF PROBLEM DRINKING

The important thing to appreciate is that there's no clear dividing line between OK drinking and problem drinking. The two often merge with each other. What may be OK drinking this time, may become problem drinking next time, and then OK again after that. But the real problem with problem drinking is that it has an awfully nasty habit of becoming more and more of a problem.

'An alcoholic is someone who drinks more than their doctor.'

ANON

So how can you tell if your OK drinking is merging into problem drinking? Well, there may be lots of different clues. It may not always be possible to put your finger on any one particular thing and say, right, that's it, I'm a problem drinker. It's more a matter of looking at different aspects of yourself – the way you drink, how it fits in with your life, how you react with other people, how it affects work or family life or friendships, what it's doing to you – and seeing these as pieces in a jigsaw, building up a picture. It may be that just a few pieces are enough to recognise the pattern, or trend, of problem drinking in your case. Or maybe many more pieces are needed to see what's really going on. But it's worth looking for the clues, and deciding for yourself, or asking someone else's opinion.

So, here are some typical pieces of the jigsaw gleaned from the experiences of thousands of people who have begun to have problems with their drinking, or a drinking problem, whichever way you want to see it. Have a look down it and check much how the jigsaw builds up for you. Remember that this is *not* a sort of 'Are you an alcoholic?' quiz. There's no score that puts you in any category. There are no categories as such. Just the jigsaw.

- looking forward to your next drink
- drinking faster than your friends
- needing a drink before a meeting or confrontation
- switching to doubles or stronger drinks for no real reason
- drinking to beat boredom
- missing meals for a drink
- drinking because you're angry
- noticing remarks about your drinking
- drinking to reward yourself
- finding yourself drinking more than a year ago
- drinking to set yourself up for the day
- drowning your sorrows
- missing your favourite programme for another drink
- drinking when your under pressure
- finding excuses to carry on drinking
- drinking to feel better
- spending too much on drink

Maybe just a few of these clues fit your jigsaw, maybe many. Maybe some more often than others. Only you and those around you can tell. Many of them would fit in just as well with OK drinking as with problem drinking. But I did say that these are *early* signs, or rather, they may be in your case. Again only you and those around can get the picture.

As problem drinking develops, there may be other more worrying changes:

- beginning to feel guilty about your drinking
- feeling embarrassed about your behaviour
- finding drink interferes with your work
- having more rows with your spouse/partner
- feeling lousy in the mornings
- keeping a secret supply of drink
- brushing with the law over drink
- losing face with friends and colleagues
- cutting up rough with the kids
- missing deadlines – too little, too late
- forgetting arrangements and appointments

- pretending you're drinking less than you really are
- suffering more bumps and bruises
- having difficulty paying your bills
- not wanting to stop drinking
- not bothering to make excuses for drinking
- not knowing what to do about your drinking

As you can see, as the jigsaw builds up, it may begin to merge with more and more of a *need* to drink, a compulsion, a dependence. Not necessarily. But it may. Many people who have had drinking problems, and those who try to help them, describe a spectrum or continuum from heavy drinking to problem drinking to dependent drinking. But it may not happen in quite such a textbook way. Perhaps the jigsaw is a better analogy. The more key pieces there are, the clearer is the picture of someone being dependent on alcohol. Or to use the word most people still use – an 'alcoholic'.

ALCOHOLIC? DEPENDENT? WHAT'S THE DIFFERENCE

Let's take 'alcoholic' first. Most people use this term to describe someone who is to all intents and purposes addicted to alcohol, like being addicted to heroin or nicotine. It's actually an American expression, invented earlier this century, when there was a vogue to regard dependence on alcohol as a disease. In a society intent on extending the rights of the individual, the notion of 'alcoholism' helped to remove the guilt and stigma attached the need to drink hard. It was certainly better than condemning the inebriate as a damnable sinner; and the mutual support organisation, Alcoholics Anonymous, did much to propagate and popularise the term and the concept behind it.

The trouble is that it gives the impression that 'alcoholics' are somehow different from the rest of us. Indeed for decades, the established medical view was that people who became alcoholics had a sort of biochemical flaw, an internal allergy, that in some way made them inevitably susceptible to the addictive clutches of alcohol. Some experts reckoned it was a genetic tendency; others a personality disorder. But the implication was always that anyone who wasn't marked out to be an alcoholic was in the clear, and that for the others, once an 'alcoholic', always an 'alcoholic'.

....

In Scotland, the admission rate for alcoholism in doctors is twice that of comparable groups. In England and Wales, deaths from alcohol-related cirrhosis among doctors are three and a half times the rate for the general population.

....

We now know this to be a false idea. Not entirely false, because there is good evidence that a few people do indeed have a genetic tendency to develop tolerance to alcohol more quickly than others, and therefore to find themselves having to drink more for the same effect. But apart from that, it's now clear that there's really nothing to distinguish the 'alcoholic' from anyone else other than the need to drink too much. And that can happen to any of us.

To dispel the myth of alcoholism, a new term was introduced in 1977 – alcohol-dependence. This refers to the fundamental feature of *needing* to drink. There have been many arguments as to whether this is a psychological need or a physical need. In other words, whether the dependent person has a purely mental compulsion to drink, or whether their body in some way craves alcohol and has to have it to fight off the withdrawal symptoms. But, again, we now know that in most cases this is an artificial distinction. The dependent person is in a chicken-and-egg situation. They focus their attention on drink (that's psychological). But as they keep drinking they become more tolerant to alcohol (that's physical). They therefore need to drink more to get the same effect (that's psychological). But as they do so, they start to get symptoms of withdrawal (that's physical). And hence feel they have to drink to feel better (that's psychological), which focuses their attention on drink. And that's where we came in.

'First the man takes a drink, then the drink takes a drink, then the drink takes a man.'

Old Japanese proverb

You'll notice I've just described a full circle of dependence – starting with a focus on drink, and finishing with more of a focus on drink. In reality, it's not so much a circle as a downward spiral – a vortex of desperation. In fact, a vortex describes it well. Becoming alcohol-dependent is rather like moving towards a whirlpool. At first the waters are slow-moving and calm, and you could swim to safety if you wanted to. But as you go round and round, you gradually get nearer and nearer to the centre of the whirlpool, and the current makes it much more difficult for you to save yourself. All too soon you're drawn to the sloping edge of the whirling cone of water, completely out of control, just managing to keep your head above the surface, until you disappear into the vertiginous abyss.

Vortex, circle, spectrum, jigsaw – I apologise for the profusion (or should I say confusion) of analogies. But I hope you see what I'm driving at. These are all ways of looking at what may be happening to you, or to someone you know. They are all ways of seeing a pattern or a trend. Of recognising that there's a problem with drink, and something needs to be done about it.

HOW TO COPE WITH PROBLEM DRINKING

OK, let's assume that you know you've got a bit of a problem with your drinking, and you've decided to tackle it. What next?

The first task is to get a measure of what you're dealing with – easier said than done. There are so many imponderables. So many side issues. So many grey areas. So many complicating factors. There always are.

But there's one aspect of the whole minefield that *is* quite easily measurable. And that's the drinking itself. What, when, where and how you drink. It's important to keep a tally of this, because not only does it focus your attention on the main problem, but it also helps you set yourself something to aim at. So the first step is to keep a drinking diary, and armed with this, you can spot the trigger situations and find ways to avoid them. What's more, by monitoring your drinking you will get an idea of what progress you're making.

1. KEEP A DRINKING DIARY ....

You may remember I described how to do this on p.28. This time it's not just for a week, but for as long as it takes to sort out the problem. It's a matter of recording enough detail to help you measure your drinking level, monitor the situations which triggered drinking, and document the consequences.

Keep a note of the day, time, place, who with, what doing, how feeling, what happened, and number of units. Unlike the unit counting diary we did earlier on in the book, with this one it's the detail in the 'who with', 'what doing', and 'how feeling' columns that's especially important for the next stage.

Keep your drinking diary for at least 12 weeks, writing in your entries as soon after drinking as possible. Don't wait until the end of the week, or until you've got nothing better to do. Accuracy and immediacy are crucial to success.

2. IDENTIFY THE TRIGGERS TO DRINKING ....

After two or three weeks, sit down with your diary and see if you can spot some recurring themes – some frequent triggers to drinking, some troublesome times, some common circumstances causing problems. Make a list of situations or feelings associated with trouble-free drinking – and those that seemed to cause problems. It may be who you were with, what you were doing, your state of mind – anything that will help you frame a strategy for coping with the trigger situations. Repeat this exercise at regular intervals. As time goes by you'll get a clearer and clearer idea of what rules you need to set yourself to beat the booze.

> *'Alcohol is in some ways worse than drug addiction, because once you're out of the drug scene you're out of it but alcohol is always around you, so therefore you have to sort of temper your way of life; you have to look to reorganise your life so that you steer yourself as far away from the temptation of alcohol as you can, because I still get tempted – I mean, there are still days when I'd love to have a pint.'*
>
> JIMMY GREAVES

---

3. DECIDE YOUR PERSONAL TEN COMMANDMENTS ....

Armed with your newfound understanding of why you do it, now set yourself some rules for controlling your drinking. Your own personal Ten Commandments about:

- which feelings or situations to be avoided
- what you will do instead
- when you will allow yourself to have a drink
- how long your sessions will last

- who to drink with and who to avoid
- where to drink and where not to
- what activity you will combine your drinking with
- what drink to choose
- how fast you will let yourself knock it back
- how many units maximum a day

As you can imagine, this last commandment – your daily maximum – is particularly important. After all, it's the bottom line.

The precise number of units you set yourself will depend a great deal on the size of your drinking problem. It's no good setting yourself an impossible goal in a fit of puritanical zeal. You'll simply get demoralised and cash your chips in. No, the best thing is to choose an achievable starting point and gradually work down from there. If possible – but bearing in mind what I've just said – try to start with the following daily maximum:

> *For men*   no more than ten units a day
> *For women*   no more than seven units a day

But remember, this isn't a recommended daily drinking level. This is the absolute *maximum* for the heaviest day of your week. You've still got to aim to keep your whole week's drinking below the 'heavy' range of warning zone (35 units or less for a man, 21 or less for a woman). So, I hope that on other days you'll drink much less, and perhaps on one or two days no alcohol at all. Miracles can happen!

But in case you need some help, here are some tips for cutting down:

- *Pace your drinking*. One of your commandments should set out how many units you will sip over what period of time.
- *Take smaller sips*. Consciously spin each drink out. See if you can make it last longer than anybody else's. Never gulp.
- *Put your glass down* between sips. If it's in your hand, it'll be in your mouth.
- *Do something else* as well. Distract yourself from drinking by doing something enjoyable – chatting, playing darts, watching telly, dancing, making love. If it takes your nose out of the glass, do it.
- *Dip out of rounds*. This is not cheating, it's being sensible. Go dutch.
- *Try a different tipple*. Choose something new and really taste it.

Analyse it with your tongue, and try to describe its subtleties.
Preferably, make it alcohol-free or low-alcohol. Become a
lemonade buff.

4. LOOK FOR ALTERNATIVES TO DRINKING...........

I won't dwell on this too long. But as you progress with the guidelines I've
been setting out, you'll hopefully find yourself being less and less tempted
into troublesome drinking situations, and more and more free to get
involved in other things. So look around for something you know you'll
enjoy doing, something you've wanted to do for quite a while but have
somehow never managed to find the time for. It may be a hobby, a sport,
a business, or just being with a special friend. Something to replace drink
as the object of your interest and attention. Something as a reward for
doing so well.

5. GET HELP WITH YOUR PROBLEMS.....................

If you're *not* doing so well, and you've still got problems, then the chances
are you're going to need some extra help. This could be your toughest
decision. It's a hard moment. It means exposing yourself – being vulnerable. But if it has to be done – and maybe only you will know that, or your
nearest and dearest – then bite the bullet you must. You must seek help.

Fortunately there's plenty about. So if you, or someone you know
and love, has reached this point, I strongly suggest you do something
about it right now.

Just talking it over with someone close, or whose guidance you
value, may be all that's needed. Perhaps your doctor or priest may be able
to help you. Or a teacher or even your boss. It depends very much on
what sort of people they are, whose side they're on, and how you feel
about them. It may just be that different way of seeing things, or alternative way of doing things, that unlocks the chains for you. Or it may
persuade you that you need further help.

So, you may find yourself seeking help from one of the many
organisations who can offer information, advice and counselling for
people who have problems linked to drink. Make good use of them. Many
have local branches, and run groups for people to share their experiences
and learn from each other. I've given a list of the main organisations and
sources of further information and help on pp.143–48.

HOW TO SURVIVE A PARTY

You're getting ready for a party. So what's the most important thing to get right? Your clothes? Your hair? Your eyes, lips or allure (whatever that is)?

Everyone has their individual preoccupations but, if you're going to be having a few drinks you'd be well advised to pay particular attention to . . . your stomach. Not holding it in, but what you're holding in it.

Drinking on an empty stomach not only sends the alcohol to your head much more quickly, it also considerably increases the likelihood that you will end the evening doubled up on your knees in front of the host's toilet-bowl. It's the headspinning effect of booze that upsets your stomach, by sending conflicting messages to the co-ordinating centre in your mid-brain. In its confusion, the brain assumes you're being tossed about on the deck of a dinghy in a Force Ten, and you dutifully throw up.

To slow down this sudden 'hit' of alcohol, the simplest pre-party trick is to line your stomach with food – any food – but protein and fats do this job best. A cheese, meat or egg sandwich might be a good idea before you go out or, if you're watching your cholesterol-count, try some baked beans, fish-fingers, or unsalted nuts. For those too lazy to think about eating, a pint of milk is a popular pre-party tipple.

Before you go it is well worth considering how much you actually want to drink over the evening. Do you want to stay pretty sober, get totally legless, or hit a happy medium? If the middle option is your answer, I suggest you skip the rest of this section and turn to the chapter on hangovers while you can still think straight.

STAYING SOBER

'One reason I don't drink, is that I want to know when I'm having a good time.'

NANCY ASTOR

Regular drinkers may initially dread the prospect of *staying sober* at a party. What could be more miserable? they ask, only to find the answer in their friends' green and gaunt faces the next day. The fact is you *can* have a good time and *not* have a hangover. Abstainers often find that, as the evening progresses, their spirits rise along with those of their drinking friends. Human beings respond to atmospheres as well as to alcohol. If people around us relax, so do we.

At every party there will be someone to tell you that by not drinking alcohol you are being anti-social or a wimp. Stick to your guns, and to your low-alcohol or soft drinks. You may be doing the unconventional thing, but they probably feel less secure about it than you do. If you need a rationale, you're not telling them what they should be drinking so why should they dictate to you? Still, you're sober and not looking for a fight. Make light of the issue. There's no need to start preaching, but no need to be apologetic about it either.

'I think. Therefore I am . . . not drinking thanks.'
MORGAN DANVERS

One of the toughest things about keeping off the booze at a party is deciding what to drink instead. Low-alcohol or alcohol-free beers and wines are getting better as far as taste is concerned, but if a swig or two only leaves you yearning for the real stuff you may be better off experimenting with fruit juices and mixers. An adventurous approach can produce some spectacular soft-drink cocktails and for once you won't suffer for having mixed your drinks!

'If you can keep your head while all about you are getting out of theirs . . . you'll be a Man, my son.'
RUDYARD KIPLING (almost!)

Besides taste, there is sometimes the additional problem of 'image'. In a macho environment, it's not easy being a hard man with a soft drink. One answer is to call your tomato juice and ice a 'Bloody Mary' or have a slice of lemon in your mineral water to make it look more gin-like. Beer drinkers can order two bottles of the low-alcohol stuff and fill a pint glass. But why bother? If you really want to be macho about it, a yard of fizzy ginger ale is considerably harder to get down in one go than a

yard of ale that's stronger but flatter. And the way some low-alcohol beers taste, only a real, real man can knock them back without wincing!

THE HAPPY MEDIUM

'It only takes one drink to get me loaded. Trouble is I can't remember whether it's the thirteenth or fourteenth.'

DEAN MARTIN

What is the secret of sensible drinking, that *happy medium* between staying sober and dancing drunkenly into your host's hi-fi? The best thing is to think about what you are going to drink and decide on what, for you, is a reasonable limit. The alcohol content of your chosen drink and the number of units you can expect in a party glassful are key factors. If you don't give yourself any guidelines, the chances are you'll end up drinking more than a 'sober you' would recommend. Of course, even if you do set yourself a limit, it can still be a battle to keep to it, as the first couple of drinks have a sneaky habit of weakening a once steely resolve! Rather than aim for a limit and then switch to soft drinks, you may prefer to drink shandies (beer and lemonade) or spritzers (wine and tonic or soda). Or again create your own distinctive half-and-half. Another variation is to alternate your drinks, taking a soft drink between each alcoholic one. In France it is common for the wine drinker to have a glass of water close at hand; since the French consume over ten times as much wine as we do in the UK, they probably know a thing or two about the subject! Alternating alcohol with water has the added bonus of lessening the dehydration which is responsible for many a morning-after headache.

A lot of people get drunk because they drink too quickly. The human liver needs about an hour to deal with each unit of alcohol consumed. In a party situation people tend to drink more than a half-pint of beer, a glass of wine or one measure of spirits in the first hour, flooding their systems with more alcohol than they are equipped to deal with. It pays to pace yourself. Are you a fast drinker? Is there something just a little automatic about the way your hand keeps raising the glass to your lips? Perhaps you sometimes notice yourself taking a sip just to fill a pause in the conversation? Thinking about your drinking habits is a useful step on the way to gaining more control. Give your liver a chance!

TIPS FOR HOSTS AND HOSTESSES

If you're hosting the party, it's in your interests to help those who are trying to control their alcohol intake. You might not want to ban the booze, but there's plenty else you can do to prevent long queues outside the loo, keep your carpet clean and your record collection unscathed! We've already talked about the way food reduces alcohol's immediate effects, and providing some for your guests will give them something else to do besides drink! It's worth remembering though, that salty snacks make us want to drink more, so crisps and nuts are not a good idea – why do you think they're the only kind of food you can get at most pubs?

Don't make the mistake of thinking that a good host is one who is constantly topping up their guests' glasses. A good host lets a drinker feel free to make up his own mind, free to ask for a change of drink when he wants it and free to say 'no' without being looked upon as a killjoy.

Make sure a fair selection of soft or low-alcohol drinks is available. For people who would rather drink booze but are trying not to, it's a bitter blow for them to find they've got to choose between orange juice, lemonade and water. You'll be amazed at the variety of really mouth-watering low-alcohol cocktails and fruit-cups you could concoct (*see* 30 Great Recipes for Drinking Without Sinking on pp.130–5), to say nothing of the many commercial low- and no-alcohol beers, ciders and wines on the market (see below). Sadly, the boffins haven't managed to come with a low-alcohol spirit yet.

> *'I think these days people look much more cool when they've got a Perrier in their hand.'*
>
> KIM WILDE

LOW-ALCOHOL AND ALCOHOL-FREE DRINKS

> *'As long as it looks like alcohol . . . just act tiddly and no one will notice!'*
>
> EDWINA CURRIE

Between August 1987 and September 1988, sales of low-alcohol (LA) and alcohol-free beers and wines roughly doubled. Sales of the hard stuff were still about one hundred times greater but, with improvements in production techniques (and taste!) and a growing recognition of the benefits of sensible drinking, the market for alcohol-free and less intoxicating alternatives will continue to expand. In fact, compared to Australia and the USA, Britain has been a bit slow to get in on the act. Drinking 'down under' may, in some minds, conjure up an abstainer's vision of hell, but the Aussie who asks for a Swan Special Light is in no danger of being laughed (or thrown) out of the bar. Random breath testing and the trend for healthy, active lifestyles have made low-alcohol beers an acceptable part of Australia's drinking culture. In the United States, it is the beers which are totally alcohol-free that have really made their mark. Their low-alcohol counterparts are struggling in a market where 'Lite' beers, 2 or 3 per cent alcohol and low in calories, are already well established.

At the moment there is no legal definition of what constitutes 'low-alcohol', but the *de facto* definition is below 1.2 per cent. Why 1.2 per cent? Well, as from May 1989, the EEC insists that all drinks with an alcohol content of over 1.2 per cent must declare their precise strength. And 1.2 per cent just happens to be the level above which Customs and Excise feel obliged to relieve you of your duty!

'Alcohol-free' or 'no-alcohol' means no more than 0.05 per cent alcohol. This is actually less than the amount that often occurs naturally in ripe fruit juice. Even a lifelong teetotaller may have traces of alcohol in the bloodstream as the result of natural fermentation in their intestines.

The distinction between a 'low-alcohol' drink and an 'alcohol-free' one is important, particularly for drivers or lunchtime drinkers with an afternoon's work still to be done. Switching to a low-alcohol beer after a pint of regular beer will continue to top up your alcohol level and may push you over the desired limit, be it the official driving limit, or a personal level of control. This will not happen if your drink is alcohol-free.

MAKING LOW-ALCOHOL DRINKS ....

This is quite a technical challenge. How to remove the alcohol without taking with it the congeners – those flavours, aromas and other attributes that give a wine, beer or cider its special character.

One method is to 'cook' it – or at least to heat the alcoholic beverage until it gives off its alcohol as distilled spirit. But this warming process alters the subtleties of the congeners left behind.

Another method is to pass the beverage over a semi-permeable membrane, which filters off the alcohol. But this method, known as reverse osmosis, often removes other substances too. Many of which have to be added again afterwards.

A third and much more promising method is modified ferment-ation, in which only a small proportion of the sugars in the brew or vat are converted to alcohol. One way of doing this is to stop the fermentation by chilling it – but this, too, can adversely affect the taste. So the latest biotechnology is now being brought to bear. Genetic engineers are close to perfecting a new strain of yeast which will impart full flavour to the drink, but only produce a fraction of the usual amount of alcohol. And because the process involves no extra stages other than fermentation, the result should be tasty without being pricey.

Whatever method is used, the fact that the alcohol is gone means that its preservative effects have been lost, and artificial preservatives or carbon dioxide may have to be added to give the drink a longer shelf-life.

De-alcoholising is currently an expensive business. What with the extra manufacturing costs, and the small, but growing, volume of the market, the end-product inevitably costs more to make and sell than its alcoholic counterpart. But brewers and winemakers are anxious to encourage sales, and are bringing prices down. The Chancellor, too, has made low-alcohol drinks relatively cheaper by increasing the duty on the full-alcohol equivalents.

LOW-ALCOHOL AND ALCOHOL-FREE BEERS ....

There are, to date, over 50 alcohol-free and low-alcohol beers on the market, the lagers outnumbering the bitters by two to one. With new brands appearing all the time, no list would dare call itself comprehensive. The following guides have been compiled with the kind assistance of the Brewers' Society.

LAGER

Brand Name	% Alcohol	Brand Name	% Alcohol
Alsator Low Alcohol Beer	0.8	Pilz Low Alcohol	0.3
Barbican	Nil	Prohibition	0.6
Bavarian Brew	1.0	Prostel	0.5
Birell	0.9	Prostel Continental	Nil
Carlton Courage	0.9	Royal Lite	0.8
Carlton Special Light	0.9	Scandia LA	0.9
Clausthaler LA	0.5	Schutz Lite	0.9
Clausthaler Special	0.6	Spar LA	0.3
Danish Light	0.9	St Christopher	Nil
Dansk LA	1.2	Stralauer	0.5
Edelbrau	1.0	Swan Special Light	0.9
Germania	0.8	Talisman	0.9
Gerstel	0.8	Tennents LA	0.9
Kaliber	Nil	Warteck Low Alcohol	0.5
McEwans LA	0.9	Weizenthaler	0.45
Panther	0.9	Zero	Nil
Patrizier Zero	Nil		

BITTER

Those who like their bitter served at a soothing room temperature may be justified in asking why so many LA bitters have 'Serve Chilled' printed on the bottle. It is well known that a long spell in the fridge can make a ropey bottle of wine taste a little less ropey; are the brewers hoping similar tactics will mask the taste of their LA products? Who knows, but if you like your beer warm, drink the LAs that way and make up your own mind. There are some fine-tasting LA and alcohol-free bitters out there, believe me!

Brand Name	% Alcohol	Brand Name	% Alcohol
Badger LA	0.9	Greenalls LA	0.9
Bass LA	1.0	Highway	0.9
Eagle LA Bitter	0.9	John Hop	1.0

Brand Name	% Alcohol	Brand Name	% Alcohol
Legend LA	<1.2	Strait	0.9
Lowes	1.0	Wheelright	1.0
Maxim Light	0.9	White Label	1.0
Pilgrims	0.9	Wyvern	1.0
Randall's LA	0.9	Youngs Extra Light	1.0
Smithwicks AFB	Nil		

CIDER

Strongbow LA was the first low-alcohol cider to come on the market, its taste lying somewhere between the full strength Strongbow and the sweeter Woodpecker. Worth a try, as are the other three listed below.

Brand Name	% Alcohol	Brand Name	% Alcohol
Cidre Stassen	0.3	Marcle Orchard	1.0
Coates Somerset Light Alc.	0.9	Strongbow LA	0.9

WINES

The winemakers face a much tougher challenge than the brewers. It seems to be much more difficult to recreate the subtleties of good wine with a low-alcohol content than it is to come up with an acceptably bitter bitter, or light and lively lager.

Check the label! It is worth remembering that the alcohol content of some LA wines, though less than standard wine, may still be between 3 and 5 per cent. If you were to drink these wines by the pint, the effect would be similar to drinking regular beer, so don't get too carried away!

Brand Name	% Alcohol	Brand Name	% Alcohol
Ariel	<0.5	Marcel Boclais	<0.5
Belmont Light	3.0	Masson Light	<0.5
Carl Jung	Nil	Miranda Sangria	5.0
Chais Clair	5.0	Monteverdi	3.0
Eisberg	Nil	Perino	5.0
Escoubes Light	2.5	Petillant de Listel	2–3.0
Fioretti Lambrusco	4.5	Seagers Classic	3.5
Giacobazzi Lambrusco	3.0	Sichel Light	<0.5
Goldener Oktober Light	2.0	Sonnenburg	<0.5
Graeff Light	0.5	Tesco Lambrusco Light	<0.5
Graeff Semi Light	4.5	Tesco Riesling	<0.5
Hans Barth	0.5	Toselli Spumante	<0.5
Konigsburg	<0.5	Wunderbar	<0.5
Lowenwein	<0.5		

30 GREAT RECIPES FOR DRINKING WITHOUT SINKING

Here are thirty low-alcohol and alcohol-free cocktails you might like to try.

Cinderella

Equal parts of orange juice, lemon juice, and pineapple juice. Serve with ice.

Parson's Particular

Two parts orange juice, one part lemon juice. Beat in one egg white and a few dashes of grenadine. Serve with ice.

Mint Fizz

4 tablespoons chopped mint
1 teaspoon sugar
250ml orange juice
125ml boiling water
juice of one lemon
250ml soda water
a little extra mint for decoration

Mix mint with sugar, and add boiling water. Leave to cool. Strain liquid into mixed juices and ice. Add soda water, decorate with mint.

Spice o' Life

250ml orange juice
125ml pineapple juice
100ml lime cordial
juice of ½ lemon
250ml water
4 cloves
1 teaspoon cinnamon
1 teaspoon mixed spice
250ml ginger ale

Warm all ingredients in a pan, except for ginger ale. Pour into a jug and leave to cool. Strain, add ginger ale and ice.

Shirley Temple

250ml ginger ale
1 teaspoon grenadine
ice

Decorate with a slice of orange, a slice of lemon, cherries, animal crackers, etc.

Arcadia

250ml apple juice
juice of one lemon
1 teaspoon chopped mint
ice

Basil Fawlty

250ml tomato juice
juice of ½ lemon
1 tablespoon chopped basil

Oasis

2 teaspoons honey
1 teaspoon ground coriander
250ml water
a slice of cucumber

Gently warm honey and water in a pan, stir in coriander and leave to cool. Add ice and decorate with cucumber.

Heavy Breather

250ml tomato juice
125ml grapefruit juice
½ teaspoon crushed garlic
1 tablespoon natural yoghurt
Worcester sauce to taste

Mix ingredients and leave to stand for half an hour. Serve with ice.

Red Alert

Equal parts of low-alcohol red wine, tomato juice, and tonic water. Serve with ice and a slice of lemon. Worcester sauce to taste.

Citrus punch

250ml orange juice
125ml pineapple juice
125ml grapefruit juice
juice of one lemon
500ml tonic water

Mix fruit juices. Add tonic water just before serving.

Pinky 'n' Perky Punch

1 bottle (70cl) low-alcohol rosé
250ml lemonade
125ml raspberry syrup
125ml lime cordial
1 lemon, thinly sliced

Ginger Tingler

1 part apple juice
2 parts ginger beer
a sprinkle of ground nutmeg

Red Eye

1 part tomato juice
1 part low-alcohol lager

Serve straight or on the rocks.

Cucumber Cool

1 large cucumber
100ml natural yoghurt
100ml lemonade
1 tablespoon chopped chives

Refrigerate ingredients (except chives) before use. Put cucumber through a blender, mix in the yoghurt, lemonade and chives, and serve immediately.

Autumn Fizz

250ml low-alcohol sparkling white wine
100ml apple juice
a dash of ginger ale
a slice of apple for decoration

Brighton Breezy

200ml pineapple juice
200ml soda water
juice of half a lemon
2 teaspoons grenadine

Ditchwater

1 part pineapple juice
1 part grapefruit juice
2 parts cola
ice

Don't be put off by the colour!

Megabite

250ml tomato juice
100ml lime cordial
a dash of Tabasco (not too much!)

Bugs Bunny

250ml carrot juice
250ml tomato juice
juice of half a lemon
a dash of orange juice
1 teaspoon parsley

Mix ingredients. Ice and lettuce optional.

Frostbite

1 part lemon juice
1 part lime cordial
4 parts crushed ice
2 parts milk
sugar to taste

Shake ingredients and strain into glasses.

Petillant Punch

1 bottle low-alcohol sparkling wine
700ml ginger ale
400ml red grape juice

Serve with fruit slices and ice.

Bitter Sweet

1 part pineapple juice
1 part bitter lemon
a dash of Angostura bitters

Serve with ice and a slice of lemon.

Sunset Boulevard

400ml grapefruit juice
100ml lime cordial
1 teaspoon grenadine syrup

Green Goddess

4 parts tonic water
1 part mint syrup

Serve chilled, with a green cherry.

The Staying Dry Martini

5 parts tonic water
1 part lime cordial

Serve with ice, lemon and a green olive. Wait a short while, to allow the
flavours to mix, before drinking.

Bicks Fuzz

1 part orange juice
1 part low-alcohol sparkling white wine

A Bucks Fizz for anyone on the wagon, or about to drive one. Be careful what you call it!

Milk Maid

200ml milk
100ml apple juice
100ml orange juice
1 teaspoon lemon juice
1 teaspoon honey

Whisk ingredients together and leave to stand for half an hour, then chill in the fridge. Serve with slices of orange and apple.

Heaven Scent

400ml cold tea
100ml ginger ale
juice of one lemon

Mix lemon juice and tea, adding sugar to taste. Add ginger ale and ice just before serving. Decorate with mint and lemon slices.

Mousehattan

A Manhattan without the alcohol. Take a clean, stemmed glass, and add one whole cherry. Try to make it last.

CHAPTER FIFTEEN

HEADQUAKE!

You know all about it even before you wake up ... The wall-to-wall brainpain. The gut-grinding nausea. The throat-tearing thirst. The socket-scraping eyeballs. The never-never-NEVER-again desolation. It all adds up to the living hell of a helluva hangover. But why should one of life's great pleasures have such a vicious sting in the tail?

The moralists will murmur about just desserts and divine retribution. But the real reason is that alcohol, and various other chemicals in drink, have a literally poisonous effect on the central nervous system.

'Intoxicated' is Latin for 'pierced with a poison dart', and those Roman soaks knew what they were talking about. Hi-tech biochemistry has revealed that, as well as alcohol, there are scores of other organic substances in many alcoholic drinks, mostly products of fermentation and maturation processes.

Alcohol itself is a strong dehydrating agent. In order for the liver to break it down, each molecule of ethyl alcohol uses up to eight molecules of water. So, as far as the body is concerned, alcohol is like blotting paper, sucking water out of the tissues, and then releasing it as extra urine. In other words it acts as a diuretic.

The brain registers its protest in a number of ways. Firstly, it tells you you're thirsty – a rasping message from the thirst-monitoring centre in your hypothalamus. Secondly, cerebral irritation jiggers up the pain sensors in the linings of your brain. And thirdly, pain-sensitive blood vessels coursing over your cortex dilate and stretch, so that each beat of your pulse feels like the clanging of a thousand dustbin lids.

'I feel as if somebody stepped on my tongue with muddy feet.'

W. C. FIELDS

But what really wracks those beleaguered blood vessels is the toxic effect of the many other organic chemicals, present in tiny but powerful amounts in most drinks. As well as ethyl alcohol, there may be related types of alcohol – such as methyl alcohol (aka meths), which in larger quantities can cause blindness and madness – aldehydes, such as formaldehyde, used for embalming corpses – and ketones, such as acetone, used to remove nail-varnish. There are also tannins (that make bitter bitter, and dry wine drier), anthocyanins (the red in red wine and port), catechins (that give character to malt whiskies), and many other phenolic flavonoids that impart the subtleties of colour and flavour so beloved of wine-buffs, beer-freaks and Scotch-scoffers.

In the business, these substances are rather quaintly known as 'congeners' – but their effects are often far from congenial. When they reach the brain they start to irritate the blood vessels and other tissues, triggering a kind of inflammation with symptoms similar to meningitis, except that it's caused by chemicals rather than bugs. Once the sedative and anaesthetic effects of the alcohol have worn off, usually after about six to eight hours, you're left fully exposed to the evils of these congeners.

As with so many other bodily functions, the human metabolism can at least partly adapt to changing circumstances. It 'learns' to deal with the toxic substances it is repeatedly exposed to by developing the particular enzymes needed to break them down. This 'tolerance' takes days, weeks or months to occur, depending on which enzymes and chemical processes are involved.

People vary a great deal in their tolerance of the alcohol and congeners in drink. Seasoned drinkers, especially those who tend to stick to their favourite tipple, often handle such substances quite well. Their metabolism adjusts to detoxify them more quickly, and their tissues are less sensitive to the effects. But the occasional or social drinker, or someone who enjoys a wide variety of drinks, has a metabolism that's rather less ready and willing to grapple with these gremlins, because the necessary enzymes aren't around in enough quantity.

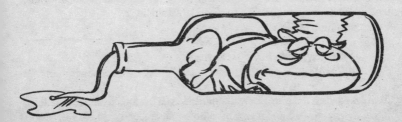

And mixing drinks – the 'grape' with the 'grain' for instance – can create a whole new set of compounds which can completely confuse the chemistry, and more or less guarantee hours of real purgatory.

The site of all this detoxification is the liver, the body's chemical plant. And although a trained liver can deal with alcohol and congeners more quickly, there's a flip-side to the equation – each time it does so, it dies a little. As I've said, these substances are poisons, and they can damage cells. The liver cells are very much in the front line, and are particularly vulnerable – hence the risk of cirrhosis. And once enough of its cells are damaged or destroyed, the liver's ability to detoxify substances is reduced. This means that people with damaged livers can't handle their drink so well – their blood alcohol levels are higher, they are more intoxicated, and their remaining liver cells face an even tougher task. Hence the urgent need for them to stop drinking.

So much for the autopsy, but what can you do to minimise the damage, or better still, avoid a hangover in the first place?

THE NIGHT BEFORE

Well, firstly, it makes sense to watch what you're drinking. Obviously the alcohol content is an important factor, and I've gone into all that on pp.38–9. But the essential thing is to curb those congeners – and this means knowing which drinks have less of them, and which have more. In other words, which drinks are boozer-friendly, and which aren't.

Just to make things easy, here's my Richter Scale of Headquake Force:

Vodka	**Force 1**	Most boozer-friendly
Gin, Champagne	**Force 2**	
White wine	**Force 3**	
Beer, Lager	**Force 4**	
Scotch, White rum	**Force 5**	
Sherry, Vermouth	**Force 6**	
Red rum, Madeira	**Force 7**	
Red wine	**Force 8**	
Brandy, Liqueur	**Force 9**	
Port, Bourbon	**Force 10**	Least boozer-friendly

Needless to say, the drinks with the lowest Headquake Force are least likely to give you a hangover; and diluting any alcoholic drink with a soft mixer or water will reduce its Force.

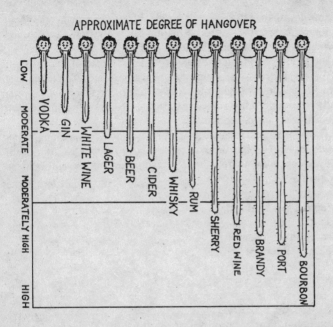

APPROXIMATE DEGREE OF HANGOVER

Certainly just about the single most effective thing you can do to avoid a headache is to down a pint of water before you go to bed. It not only dilutes the congeners but also counteracts the dehydrating diuretic effect of alcohol. Force yourself if necessary – but get that water inside you before you slump into a stupor, because it's easily the best antidote there is. However much you may hate it.

> 'Germs lie in wait in it,
> Larvae pupate in it,
> Dead fish stagnate in it,
> Frogs fornicate in it,
> So flush the damn stuff down the drain.'
>
> PETER CHRISTIE

But what if, by some oversight, you fail to imbibe the necessary liquid, and lo and behold, you emerge next morning with a real humdinger of a hangover? What can you do about it? Well, the best thing you can do is go back to sleep again. Time is a great healer of hangovers, and so is unconsciousness. An extra hour or so of oblivion can make the living death a lot more bearable – especially if you can throw down a toothmugful or two of water before you submerge again.

But a long lie-in isn't always possible. A sense of duty, fear of reprisal, or sheer force of habit may drag you from your sickbed and prod you through the pain-wracked routine of getting off to work. This is when you really need help – how to survive, and even try to function, with a cranium-crunching mega-headquake.

The first thing to remember, if you can remember anything, is that it can be done. People have survived these things. There *is* life after death. So don't just mope about groaning. You can tackle your hangover in any of five main ways:

- replace lost fluid
- soothe the pain
- speed up the chemistry
- perk up the spirits
- calm the nerves

REPLACE LOST FLUID ....

Again you could drink a lot of water – and that's a LOT of water. Tap water would do, but fizzy is better. The tang on the tongue has a re-vitalising effect far greater than any supposed medicinal value. Carbonated water (soda water) or fizzy mineral water can do an excellent job, especially along with plenty of ice and lemon. There are lots of fizzy mineral waters (either naturally gassy or artificially carbonated), and although there are discernable taste differences between them, from a head-clearing point of view, they're all as good as each other.

Fruit juice – any fruit juice – in bulk, is also good. So, too, is tea, if you like tea – and it helps to like it because you'll be drinking it by the potful. Milk is usually not such good news – it tends to make your queasiness turn vindictive.

SOOTHE THE PAIN ....

With a painkiller, yes – but which one? Aspirin would work well enough, but it irritates the stomach, and right now you don't much want your stomach irritated. It's better to take paracetamol – one or two tablets, no more than four-hourly. But do NOT be tempted to exceed this dose; paracetamol can be quite cruel to the liver, and yours won't be in any great shape to fight back.

SPEED UP THE CHEMISTRY ....

Most of the detoxification going on in the liver consists of complex metabolic processes that can be helped along by taking extra vitamin C (either as fruit juice, preferably freshly squeezed oranges or lemons, or as effervescent vitamin C tablets). The chemistry can also be given a nudge with fructose – a form of sugar found in various fruits, but most abundantly in honey.

Another way to speed things up is to take in as much oxygen as you decently can. This could simply mean some deep long breaths of fresh air. But if you're really serious about blowing your hangover away, it's hard to beat a ten- or fifteen-minute run. It's even harder to get out there and do it – but that's beside the point.

PERK UP THE SPIRITS ....

Much of the abject gloom and despondency hanging over you can be dispelled with that other favourite drug – caffeine. In tea, coffee or cola drinks, caffeine is a stimulant and can do wonders in raising the spirits. But many people find they simply can't face any of these drinks when they're hung over, even without milk. And although a cup of strong tea or coffee may make you feel a lot brighter, don't make the well-known mistake of thinking that it sobers you up in terms of your alcohol level. In fact, it will make not a jot of difference to your blood alcohol concentration (BAC), and won't fool the breathalyser one little bit!

CALM THE NERVES ....

Alcohol is a sedative and anaesthetic, and it does that by making brain cells less reactive, less responsive – very laid back indeed. Unfortunately, when this effect wears off a few hours later, the brain cells feel the pinch and become extremely irritable and twitchy, causing the hyper horrors of a hangover – the slightest sound deafens you, light scythes into your skull, and pain hangs, draws and quarters you.

'Dear Alka Seltzer, please can you make your tablets quieter?'

MORGAN DANVERS

Technically, what's happening is that your brain cell membranes have become destabilised and hyperexcitable by withdrawal of alcohol. Hence the rationale for the 'hair of the dog' – another drink of alcohol – to help restore some sort of calm and order.

Of course, there's a snag to this apparently foolproof remedy. More alcohol means more of the very substance that can cause so much trouble – and once you get into the habit of using alcohol to help you cope with the downside of using alcohol, you're teetering on the edge of a very slippery slope indeed.

'Take the juice of two quarts of whisky . . .'
EDDIE CONDON

If you often feel you need a drink to get you out of the black hole you've fallen into with your previous drink, then you are likely to be sliding into the much bigger and blacker hole of alcohol-dependence. What may be happening to you is that you are becoming dependent on alcohol to get over its effects. If you think this may be true in your case, I strongly suggest you turn to Chapter 13 for some advice which could help you.

But having said all that, there's no evidence to suggest that the *moderate* drinker, with the *occasional* hangover, is risking alcohol-dependence by having a *little* alcohol before lunch the following day (even I, with my relatively tolerant attitude to drink, would bridle at the idea of alcohol before breakfast).

A little alcohol in a long fresh drink can undoubtedly do wonders for raw nerves. Used sparingly and selectively, the hair of the dog can have a lot going for it. After all, there are some rather pleasant hairs of the dog around. My own favourite is a Bloody Mary.

Only occasionally, mind!

USEFUL ADDRESSES AND TELEPHONE NUMBERS

NATIONAL ORGANISATIONS

ENGLAND & WALES

Alcohol Concern
305 Grays Inn Road
London WC1X 8QF
Tel: 01 833 3471

Alcohol Concern is a national charity with three main aims: to raise public awareness of the problems alcohol can cause, to try to improve services for people who are drinking too much, and to promote preventive action at a local and national level. Anyone supporting these aims can become a member. It has a comprehensive library, provides leaflets and information and produces a bi-monthly journal. This guide has been compiled with their kind assistance.

Health Promotion Authority for Wales
Brunel House (8th Floor)
2 Fitzalan Road
Cardiff CF2 1EB
Tel: 222 472472

The main government-funded health information, education and campaigning body for Wales.

Institute of Alcohol Studies
Alliance House
12 Caxton Street
London SW1M 0QS
Tel: 01 222 5880

An independent body which publishes information, education and research material; provides courses and seminars from industrial alcohol programmes to alcohol control policies; has a quarterly journal, monthly digest, library and study centre.

Triple A (Action on Alcohol Abuse)
3rd Floor, Livingstone House
11 Carteret Street
London SW14 9DL
Tel: 01 222 3454

Triple A is a pressure group on alcohol policy issues and provides an information service. It produces a range of briefing papers and publishes a bi-monthly review.

Health Education Authority
Hamilton House
Mabledon Place
London WC1
Tel: 387 9528

The HEA is the main government-funded body in the field of health education. It sponsors alcohol education programmes and produces booklets such as 'That's the Limit' and posters.

SCOTLAND

Scottish Council on Alcohol
147 Blythswood Street
Glasgow G2 4EN
Tel: 041 333 9677

The Scottish Council on Alcoholism is the national body in Scotland dealing with all aspects of alcohol-related problems, with a network of 25 affiliated Councils.

Scottish Health Education Group
Woodburn House
Canaan Lane
Edinburgh EH10 4SG
Tel: 031 447 8044

SHEG is the national agency for health education and the promotion of

health in Scotland. It is entirely government funded and is part of the
NHS. One of the group's major priorities is its alcohol education and
prevention programme.

NORTHERN IRELAND . . . .

Northern Ireland Council on Alcohol
40 Elmwood Avenue
Belfast BT9 6AZ
Tel: 0232 664434

Provides information and advice on all aspects of alcohol, and co-
ordinates local action.

SELF-HELP ORGANISATION WITH LOCAL GROUPS
. . . .

Alcoholics Anonymous

A fellowship of nearly 2000 groups in the UK. Members meet to share
experiences and help each other to solve their common problem. Details
of your nearest group are available from the following sources.

England 01 352 3001
    or
General Service Office of Alcoholics Anonymous, GB
PO Box 1
Stonebow House
Stonebow
York Y01 2NJ

Wales 0222 373771 (Cardiff) 7pm–10pm
    or
09945 282 (Pendine, W Wales)

Scotland AA
Baltic Chambers
50 Wellington Street
Glasgow G2
Tel: 041 221 9027

N Ireland AA
Central Office
152 Lisburn Road
Belfast BT9 6AJ
Tel: 0232 681084

Eire AA
109 South Circular Road
Leonard's Corner
Dublin 8
Tel: 0001 538998

Al-Anon Family Groups
61 Great Dover Street
London SE1 4YF
Tel: 01 403 0888

Al-Anon is a fellowship for relatives and friends of problem drinkers, with over 850 groups in Great Britain. Members meet in confidence, share experiences and learn how to cope with problems which arise, whether the alcoholic is still drinking or in recovery.

Al-Ateen is part of Al-Anon especially for teenagers who have an alcoholic parent or other close relative.

Turning Point
CAP House
9/12 Long Lane
London EC1A 9HA
Tel: 01 606 3947

A national charity with 23 projects throughout the country, which offers information, counselling and residential facilities to people with drug and alcohol problems.

Aquarius
3rd Floor, The White House
111 New Street
Birmingham B2 4EU
Tel: 021 632 4727

This is a charity based in the West Midlands which runs a number of projects offering counselling, residential and day care facilities to people with drug and alcohol problems.

Drinkwatchers
200 Seagrave Road
London SW6 1RQ
Tel: 01 381 3155/2112

Drinkwatchers helps heavy drinkers or those worried about their drinking to reduce their consumption to sensible levels. It is not intended for those who are dependent on alcohol and who wish to abstain totally. There are 20 branches around the country.

Drinkwatchers also provides education on sensible drinking habits to young people and employees in high-risk occupations.

ACCEPT
200 Seagrave Road
London SW6 1RQ
Tel: 01 381 3155

A national charity providing education, prevention, training, treatment and research in the field of addictions – alcohol, tranquillisers and drugs.

ACCEPT runs a number of multi-disciplinary treatment centres for problem drinkers, tranquilliser misusers and their families. They also provide information, organise training courses, and are engaged in a number of joint research projects.

Salvation Army
101 Queen Victoria Street
London EC4P 3EP
Tel: 01 236 5222

The Salvation Army runs a number of projects (particularly hostels) for homeless people; they also provide some detoxification centres.

Lawyers' Support Group
c/o Flat 1, Stoneham House
13 Queen's Road
Richmond
Surrey TW10 6JW
Tel: 01 940 9163

An informal group of recovering alcoholic lawyers who are willing to make themselves available in confidence to lawyers who need help with a drinking problem or cross-addiction to other drugs.

Doctor and Dentists Group
c/o The Medical Council on Alcoholism
1 St Andrew's Place
London NW1 4LB
Tel: 01 487 4445

A contact point for doctors and dentists who may have a drink-related problem and those who can provide support and help.

INDEX

In the following index, 'alcohol' is abbreviated to 'al.'